FROM JOURNEYS TO WORDS

From Journeys to Words

Wobbly Tales of ~~Expert Wives~~ Expat Lives

PEARL
KASUJJA-VAN DE VELDE
&
JULIE
EPENU-ROBERT

FOREWORD BY
PADDY SIYANGA-KNUDSEN

ISBN: 979-10-699-7945-1 (Paperback)

Cover Design by Gareth Southwell
Formatted for paperback and e-book by Gareth Southwell

DEDICATIONS

PEARL:

To Gerd, Ava and Tes –
the best travel buddies and the loves of my life.

To Maama Mauricia and late Taata Aurelian –
without you, there would be no journeys.

JULIE:

To my adventure and life partners;
Jean-François, Nicolas and Roxanna.

To my dear mum Beatrice and my late dad Nathan.

CONTENTS

FOREWORD

PADDY SIYANGA-KNUDSEN

MILLIONS OF PEOPLE leave their homes in search of better livelihoods, for education opportunities, for family reunions or to seek refuge from political turmoil and conflict.

About 14 years ago, I left Zambia to join my husband on a new work adventure in neighbouring Tanzania – and our expatriate journey commenced.

Making that decision to venture out of my comfort zone was not easy. It meant peeling away from a close-knit extended family, good friends, a great job, busy social calendar and a delightful country. I learnt, as the years and moves went by, that adapting to change is easier said than lived.

While it may look like all rose petals on a red carpet, expat life has some real rough bits of "lost", "curious", "emotional", "exciting", "adventurous" and "unknown". It takes you to a place where you feel *mdogo kama piriton* (*small like a Piriton tablet*) – but you thrive and grow. We pack, unpack, find new schools, discover new culinary tastes, explore work options, experiment with hairdressers (one of our top priorities as

African women) and make new friends – then press 'repeat' every couple of years.

I think back to who I was before leaving Zambia: young, energetic, *sans enfant*, curious and excited about our journey as two newly-weds.

Today, apart from growth spurts in my professional life, I am now a mother to two kids, I speak more languages than I knew 14 years ago, I now know that coffee tastes the same in Kosovo and in Malaysia, I've learnt (and dreamed in) Swahili while still trying to perfect my Mandarin. I learnt that true friends come, grow with you and only go out of sight – but not out of mind. I've learnt that my faith in God grows with every challenge and every adaption I have to make.

When I miss home (Zambia), I often find myself missing other pieces of the years lived away from home. I wander off into memories of cities and markets, moments with people and cultures that I have experienced and carry with me.

I met Pearl in Beijing, China and we hit it off immediately. She later introduced me (online) to her friend Julie. While I am yet to meet Julie, Pearl said to me, "you two will just click" and we did click through similar personalities and stories – and a lot of humour.

I feel privileged to share these few reflections in this book. Their shared tales are intriguing, raw, lived experiences that I and many other expats can relate to.

Enjoy.

DISCLAIMER

WE ARE NEITHER travel ~~expats~~ experts nor the perfect Stepford Wives so this is not a travel or marriage guide. All travel recounts are strictly personal experiences, thoughts and opinions meant for pleasure-leisure reading and do not reflect a village consensus.

Some names of people described in this book have been altered to protect their privacy.

Travelling; it leaves you speechless, then turns you into a storyteller.

— IBN BATTUTA

1

WELCOME ABOARD

NEW LANDINGS, NEW COUNTRIES

We are seasoned travellers. But we do not travel for tourism which is usually the safe, controlled travel that is all planned down to a 'T'. We do not travel to have a nice vacation somewhere before going back to our 'cushy' homes. We do not travel because we are restless or we seek adventure.

No.

We pack up our houses and our entire lives and move to new countries for work – or to be precise, our other halves' work.

We are constantly disoriented strangers in new countries and cultures, seeking hospitality with our hosts, our nerves tested over and over again with the need to adapt, adjust and cope with our transient 'surroundings'.

The past 20 years have seen both of us pack up and move with our families to more than ten countries, cities and schools. Our children have thrived in an international environment, with their friends coming from almost every corner of the world.

Although we have been constantly pushed out of our comfort zones, we have bloomed in ways we never expected and the experiences we have gained from these journeys are priceless.

Join us on this unique adventure.

Pearl

Dhaka, Bangladesh – "The Desh" (2014–2016)

"LADIES AND GENTLEMEN, please sit down, fasten your seat belts, all mobile devices have to be switched off before take-off and landing ..."

If you have travelled by air, chances are you are familiar with these pre-flight announcements over the aircraft PA system. Most of us follow these simple rules. Now, our flight to Dhaka was not *most of us*.

Before moving to Bangladesh, I had been living in (my husband's home country) Belgium for almost four years where I had given birth to our first daughter and had learned a few words of that *shuuushhhhy*-sounding guttural language called Dutch (aka Flemish). When our baby turned two, my husband's employer informed him that he was being relocated to Bangladesh and naturally, our daughter and I would be moving there with him. I will admit that I cried, but tears of happiness they weren't. Dhaka had never been on my bucket list of cities to visit, let alone live in. But here we were, packing up and ready to call it our new temporary home.

Travelling from Brussels, Belgium with Qatar Airways, we arrived in Doha in the middle of the night. There, we had a four-hour layover before heading to our gate for the flight to Dhaka. And that's when the comics started.

Now, I grew up in Uganda where it was rather normal for us as kids to stare at 'strangers' (read 'white people'). But even with this childhood memory, it still came as a big shock to be stared at up, down, sideways, back, and then some more by the majority Bangladeshi passengers at our boarding gate. The situation was exacerbated by the fact that my husband is white and our daughter is a 'combo' colour. Some people simply couldn't understand this colour 'phenomenon' and came straight up and touched our daughter's hair with fascination. Oh boy! In the beginning, I smiled and tried to be polite but after a while it got a bit tiresome.

Soon, the bus taking us to the aircraft arrived. We were told to make an orderly line; you know, families with kids first, or seat numbers 20–40 first. That's when I got my second lesson about Bangladeshis; orderly queues (or any queues for that matter) don't exist. Jostling for any available space is the order of the day and the best jostler wins. I could see the airport check-in staff simply giving up.

Once inside the aircraft, some people just casually found an empty seat and sat right down with a sigh, taking their shoes off and making themselves comfortable, until of course, the person with that seat number came over and the shoeless passenger had to move – shoes, socks and carry-on luggage in hand – to his or her rightful place. It was amusing, to say the least.

Take off time was near. Obeying pre-flight safety instructions? Not happening on this flight. Some chaps continued (loudly) making phone calls with the aircraft already in the air.

On arrival in Dhaka, we were greeted by a scourge of mosquitoes like nothing I'd seen before. I was born in Africa where mosquitoes are like some relatives; annoying, but a part of us. However, mosquitoes in Dhaka seemed much bigger and more aggressive than those I was accustomed to in Uganda.

We cleared immigration – amidst more staring – and quickly located our assigned driver who so warmly welcomed us to the country and led us outside. It was scorching hot and it wasn't even 8am yet. There was an endless sea of people, cars, bicycles, rickshaws and Compressed Natural Gas (CNG) tuk-tuks, all trying to come to or depart from the Arrivals area.

Right opposite the Arrivals hall pick-up point was a fenced-off barrier with yet more people who looked like they were just spending a lazy afternoon at the airport STARING at all the incoming passengers.

Standing in the sweltering heat, we waited for our assigned car to drive nearer to where we were. However, the driver got stuck in a mini 'jam' a few metres away from us and it took over 30 minutes before he reached us and we finally loaded our eight suitcases, three bags of hand luggage, a baby pram, and an exhausted baby into the vehicle. As I would later learn, half an hour of waiting in traffic was not that bad in the (Dhaka) grand scheme of things.

We cruised out of the airport and immediately joined a roundabout that was at a complete standstill. No movement AT ALL, just a gridlock of chaotic and loudly hooting cars going absolutely nowhere. The hooting! Heavens to Betsy, the hooting in Dhaka is deafening! It seems like drivers in Dhaka simply keep their palms pressed on the car horn the entire time they are inside their vehicles – urban therapy I guess. They hoot at anything or at NOTHING at all; if there is a chicken or a bird crossing the road, or if they think it's too quiet, the horns go off. It is incessant and annoying and it is something I never got used to.

Our kind driver continued smiling and welcoming us to Dhaka.

"This is normal", he announced cheerfully. I cursed in my breath, already feeling dispirited. But we were here, we were in. No backing out, loud traffic and all.

We finally cleared the traffic motley – believe it or not, the cars and whatever else rides on the streets actually start moving at some point – and we finally arrived at our apartment that was tucked away at the end of a blind alley, overlooking Lake Banani. Life in Dhaka had begun.

First impressions on any work posting abroad are always a mixed bag of emotional uncertainty. Our three-bedroom apartment was clean and comfortable but the only furniture inside was a dining table, some chairs and beds – it felt so bare, so empty. With all the jet lag, the tiredness from the travel and the new surroundings, I was on the verge of tears. In time of course, we turned it into a comfortable home.

A day after we arrived in Dhaka, we went shopping in the local supermarket and filled up the fridge with the bare necessities. We later took a walk around the neighbourhood and discovered that Lake Banani was more of a 'pond' full of gut-churning, foetid black-green water. What bemused me though was seeing a bunch of kids happily swimming and splashing in this pond – sorry, lake – with absolutely no care in the world. In time, we realised how lucky we were to have this 'lake' view because in Dhaka, buildings are constructed so close to each other you can literally shake hands with a neighbour from the building next door. We appreciated that we didn't have a block of flats in our immediate view.

With temperatures almost always in the high 30's (°C), we were tempted to open our windows and doors for some fresh air. Well, for a long time, we couldn't because of the mozzies (mosquitoes) and the unpleasant smell emanating from the lake. After a year of acclimatising however, we just happily sat on the balcony with friends and enjoyed the lake view while sipping on some wine. I'm not sure if it was the effect of the wine that caused the sudden anosmia and mosquito tolerance, or if that was just a sign that we were comfortably settling in.

Having to learn a new language has been one of the unyielding challenges of relocations abroad for me. Thank goodness I didn't have to learn Bangla – we all know it isn't on the world's HAVE-TO-LEARN language list ... neither is Dutch to be honest, but that's a discussion for another day.

Many friends and relatives have asked us how the heck we managed to stay in Bangladesh. They have no way of knowing how wonderful this country is and how truly kind the people are. This experience enriched our lives beyond imagination and taught us to always look beyond the surface in order to find true beauty in any and every thing; in a place and in people. Dhaka was one of our best work postings abroad so far – and who'd have 'thunk'?

Lusaka, Zambia – "Zed" (2003–2005)

YEARS BEFORE our stint in Bangladesh, I had met and fallen in love with a Belgian man who was working in Uganda for an International humanitarian organisation. We clicked immediately but I knew that he only had a year left on his contract in Uganda so we didn't make plans, we just went with the flow. Before long, the year was over so he packed up and moved to his next work posting in Eritrea. We stayed in touch with no particular expectations. He was busy and so was I.

I was working at Kampala's then biggest model management agency (it was the only one at the time, to be fair, so of course it was the biggest). We were in the middle of an advertising boom with agencies and companies rebranding all sorts of products and services in Uganda; banks, mobile phone companies, car importers, etcetera. Our agency was quite busy booking jobs for the models as well as being invited to any and every decent launch event/party in town every other week. Not bad eh.

After several months in Eritrea however, my boyfriend announced that he was requesting his employer for a family work posting and that he really really really really wanted me to join him (OK, he didn't have to plead that much, I was already hooked).

Zambia became our first home as a couple and it was also the first time for both of us to be 'officially' living with anyone. I was a 22-year old with no idea of what living with a man entailed, let alone living in a new country.

OK, I reasoned, *I'm still in Africa. This is like home. Surely I will relate.*

I said *yes* immediately, told my mum and my boss about my relocation plans, packed my bags and off I went.

Early one morning, heavily hungover from yet another impromptu farewell party my friends had organised, I took a Kenya Airways flight from Entebbe, travelling first to Nairobi before landing in Lusaka later that afternoon. My boyfriend had arrived in Lusaka a month earlier and was already in our temporary apartment which was located just a street behind his office. As soon as we arrived at the apartment, I went straight to nap off the hangover and tiredness.

Suddenly, I was awoken by a cutting shriek from the apartment below ours; someone was screaming and crying so loudly. Turns out there was a lady who had also just arrived that morning to join her man, only to learn that he had passed away in a car accident that morning. Apparently, he had been based upcountry and was driving to Lusaka to pick her up from the airport when he lost his life. It was truly horrendous. I pray she found some peace and that she's well.

We moved from the temporary apartment into a pretty decent house in one of the good neighbourhoods in Lusaka. The house had a large garden and a small swimming pool that came in handy for half the year – the other half of the year being the winter months which got quite cold.

Our security guard had a tiny drinking problem and was always dead-out sleeping on the job. One time we came back home from dinner and for close to 20 minutes he was unable to hear our car horn because he was knocked out from the alcohol. We liked him a lot so we tolerated him. I hope he found a local Alcoholics Anonymous group.

We had friends visiting us in Lusaka, one of them being Julie, co-author of this book and one of the funniest and realest friends I have. She is a kindred spirit who has been in my life for over two decades and counting. She, like me, was embarking on her expat life with her then-boyfriend (now husband) and they paid us a visit in Lusaka before travelling on to their new work posting in Harare, Zimbabwe. Salma is a beauty queen in the real sense of the word. She was Miss Uganda 2003/2004 and she is a close friend of mine. She spent a few days with us in Lusaka. My cousin Gladys also paid us a visit from Cape Town where she was studying at University.

There were two main malls in Lusaka at the time – Arcades and Manda Hill. Here, one could go shopping in one of the big supermarkets, have a coffee and bite in one of the few cafes and restaurants, or just (window) shop in the few boutiques around. There wasn't much else to do in these malls.

Life in Zed was a bit TOO slow for me – especially during the first few months. It was not ideal for a young couple like us who, at the time, had no children and so had all the time in the world to party and socialise. Coming from the busy lifestyle I'd had in Kampala to an *easy-going* one in Lusaka made me feel rather lost (read 'bored'). It was our first test in cohabiting. I think that I was a restless soul because this new, big chapter in my life was happening away from everything and everyone I was familiar with in Uganda. I believe we didn't enjoy Lusaka as much as we should have because we were young, hungry for a faster-paced life in a faster-paced city and we were still 'discovering' each other as a couple.

The best thing about Zambia was the people – so

welcoming and kind. Visiting Victoria falls as well as the many safaris we took were true highlights of our stay in Zambia.

20 something years later and with all the Zambian friends I've made since, Zambia would be perfect for us now.

Beijing, China (2017–2021)

CHINA. The mighty giant. One of the top destinations on my bucket list. I was beyond excited to be moving to China. My only apprehension was the thought of learning yet another language after all, I was still trying to perfect my Flemish at this point. I figured though that I would be able to use some translation APPs when and if needed. So off we went.

Hours after arriving in Beijing, we met our housekeeper a.k.a *Ayi* (Ayi means 'Auntie' in Chinese). I was excited to see her and ready for her kind help in unpacking the mountain of luggage we had with us. I greeted her in English with a simple *hi*, but no answer was forthcoming from her.

Maybe she didn't understand what I said.

So, I tried again.

"How are you?"

Blank! Just a polite smile.

At this confusing point, Kat, the (English-speaking) head of housekeeping who had accompanied the Ayi explained to us that all the Ayis employed by my husband's work in China don't speak English. She said this with a stifled *I-thought-you-knew-this* chuckle.

"Wait, What?" I exclaimed, "Not a single word of English? How am I going to be able to communicate with her?"

NOPE. Not a word.

I knew then that no translation APP in the world would

help me. I wasn't just lost in translation – I was screwed in translation. I was left open-mouthed with shock. How would I possibly spend more than five hours a day with someone I couldn't communicate with? Good grace!

"Well", said Kat, bringing out some sheets of papers from her satchel bag, "Here is a printout of the standard questions you are most likely to ask her".

She jovially handed me the papers, with a satisfied smile that said *problem solved.*

These 'printout' questions and answers, in both English and Mandarin had phrases like 'please wash the white clothes separately' and 'can you please help me post this letter' – with their corresponding answers, of course.

"To use it", she volunteered further, "just point to the question you want to ask her and in reply she can point to the answer on the sheet or she can use Baidu to answer your questions".

"Sorry, what? Baidu? What or who is Baidu?" I inquired, totally confused at this point. Turns out Baidu was one of the many translation APPs around.

As postscript, she added that if these two 'genius' forms of communication failed, I could just point at something – a washing machine for example – try a few hand gestures and hope that the Ayi would understand. O.K, got it – not.

That, ladies and gentlemen, is how I lived my first three or four months in China – speaking through pantomime and other animated gestures.

My husband was at work all day. In his office, almost everyone spoke English and for those that didn't, there was always a translator. My daughter was in school all day, busy making new friends and enjoying her Grade 1. I was home with a kind, but NON-ENGLISH-SPEAKING lady. Venturing outside the apartment filled me with dread too because I couldn't understand a word in Chinese. Needless to say, I was miserable and frustrated those first few months. I was beginning to question my 'China Dream' and how I could possibly survive in Beijing. You know that saying; 'everyone smiles in the same language'? Ahhhhh, I can assure you that in China, a smile won't get you further than your front door if you don't speak any Mandarin.

With time, I went beyond the rudimentary *Ni Hao* (你好) and *Xie Xie* (谢谢) and learned colours, numbers, greetings, the weather, saying 'this' and 'that', and of course, never forgetting the pantomime – sometimes done in an exaggerated manner to drive the point home. I still looked like a clown on any given day trying to articulate a message as best I could.

For the first few months, I resisted the obvious – an urgent need to find myself a Chinese language school and learn some Mandarin. You see, learning Dutch a few years earlier had stripped me of any energy to pick up a second language. After a while though – and with constant nagging from friends and family about how *Chinese is the most widely spoken language in the world, Pearl. It will be sooooo coooooool for you to learn it,* I had no choice but to enrol in a Chinese language school.

Mandarin is as hard as [expletive]. It is not just any local lingo – 这是最难的语言. It is like brain surgery (unless you are a brain surgeon – or a Chinese of course). Now, add to that the fact that I was in my mid 30s, a mother and wife, trying to settle my family into a new country and trying to complete a degree in International Development. I barely had the time nor the brains to fit in yet another language. As soon as I started Chinese lessons however, I knew I had made a good decision. The language is intriguing and difficult in equal measure. The more it challenged me, the further I wanted to go with learning it. The tones, the strokes ... all very fascinating.

The language school – Beijing Mandarin School – was

great. I was placed in one of the best classes with a wonderful teacher, Maggie, and classmates from Ecuador, Brazil, America, Vietnam and Indonesia. That class was an excuse to laugh all morning and have dumpling-filled lunches in the afternoon. Every language class should be like this.

After two levels, I was psyched to begin with the third and was even thinking of having a go at the *Hanyu Shuiping Kaoshi* (HSK) level 3 – the Chinese International standardised test exams. Nature however decided to bless us with an unexpected but exciting pregnancy. Months after the birth of our second baby, COVID-19 hit the world and we were forced to temporarily leave Beijing and go back to Europe (Read more about this in Chapter 2)

After seven months in Europe, four quarantines, two lockdowns and, this time not with one but two children, we were finally able to go back to Beijing. With the stress of the virus, re-settling in and supporting our oldest daughter with e-Learning, the last thing I was thinking about was enrolling back into the Chinese language school. I just had to put into practice the little Mandarin I had already learned.

Notwithstanding the hard-to-learn Mandarin and biting-cold winters, living in China was a dream come true for me. To witness their rapid modern growth and experience their tradition and culture that is still weaved into their day-to-day living was such a rewarding experience. I found the majority of Chinese people super helpful, warm and generous, especially when I made effort to speak Mandarin with them. Having a baby is also a huge conversation starter with people on the streets of Beijing.

I miss it.

WE KNEW THAT FOUR YEARS was the maximum time allowed to stay in a work posting abroad. So, we knew we were leaving China in 2021. Soon, our next posting was confirmed; Beirut, Lebanon. Before we moved to Beirut, I experienced a moment of self-reflection about my expat journey and that of my husband's – his has been way longer than mine and *waaaay* more adventurous it would blow your mind.

After more than fifteen years of relocations, new apartments, new schools, evacuations due to terror attacks, having to learn different languages, meeting and sadly saying goodbye to so many people and the life-changing pandemic a.k.a COVID-19, my mind, soul, body and spirit were all screaming for a break from these changes. This, coupled with the news at the time about the poor economic and political situation in Lebanon (fuel shortages and power cuts), I was less than enthused about our move.

But sometimes we are blind to our own strengths and luck. I quickly snapped out of this introspective, self-reflective mood and realised what a great opportunity this was; a chance to discover yet another culture and another part of the world – the Middle East – a place I had not lived before. So, with an ever-supportive husband and our two daughters, I dived into some research about Lebanon, its culture and people. And what wasn't to like (apart from the fuel shortages and power cuts, that is)?

It looked like the so-called Cotê d'Azur or Paris of the Middle East still had its charm and so much more to offer. Before long I was psyched and very much looking forward to making this our new temporary home.

And so, we packed up yet again, flew from Brussels, via Frankfurt, Germany and less than five hours later at around

4am, we arrived in Beirut. My first thought was, *Power cuts? What power cuts*, because I'd expected the airport to be half-lit or in darkness. It was lit, literally.

Second thought; *People are really nice here.* We cleared customs with very friendly immigration staff, quickly got our COVID-19 tests done at the airport by an even friendlier member of staff and out we went. Driving to the apartment took all but 10 minutes, especially since it was in the dead of night/early morning with barely any traffic on the road. Power cut issues became evident though as soon as we were on the road with tunnels and most main roads in pitch blackness.

By the time we arrived at the apartment, it was clear that power outages were a serious thing. We parked in front of what was going to be our apartment building and exited the car into pitch darkness. There was no electricity and the only lights we had were the car headlamps. The driver nonchalantly handed us an envelope with the apartment keys and proceeded to take our (more than 10) suitcases out of the car. Feeling utterly lost while holding a sleepy baby in one hand and her pram in the other, I stammered, asking the driver how the heck we were supposed to take everything upstairs to the fourth floor. Luckily, the apartment concierge heard us and he woke up, switched the power generator on and helped us load the luggage into the elevator. No sooner had we managed to get ourselves and the luggage into the new apartment than the generator was switched off again. Having grown up in Uganda, power cuts aren't something new to me. However, in a country that you have no clue about, it can be quite exasperating to be welcomed in this manner.

Whenever we travel, whether on holiday, back to Uganda or Belgium or when relocating to a new country, I make it a point to unpack as soon as we arrive. I sort out laundry, fold and put clothes away and so forth – no matter how long the trip was, how tired I feel or whether it's 2am or 11pm. It's an obsession that irks my husband. On this relocation however, I had not a single ounce of energy to unpack, especially since that meant I'd be doing it in the dark. So, we all jumped into one bed and immediately dozed off.

The following day – or rather later that day – I managed to unpack a few things, check our new home out and arrange the kids' bedrooms. We were in self-isolation inside the apartment for a few days while awaiting the results of the COVID-19 tests we had taken at the airport upon arrival. Mercifully, we had the internet so we kept the kids entertained with some Netflix while we arranged things around the apartment.

Soon, evening swung by and we needed dinner. I always carry snacks, bread, cereals, baby food and other quick bites when we travel so normally, our breakfast is sorted for the first few days of arrival in a country – but not dinner. For this, the office usually gives us a small cash advance in local currency so that we are able to buy some food and groceries from the local supermarkets. We had already installed all the important Lebanon APPs on our phones, including food delivery services. So, we ordered a Kentucky Fried Chicken (KFC) bucket to share for dinner. It was pretty easy to order and the food was delivered within minutes. On looking at the bill however, we gasped. It was 400,000 Lebanese Pounds, which, according to the official rate, was $250 (US dollars). I thought they had made a mistake because surely, not even gold-crusted chicken can cost $250. The delivery guy assured us it was 400,000LL, not 40,000LL. We ate that chicken in silence, contemplating how the heck we were going to be able to afford living in a place this expensive.

The next day, my husband called the office to clarify if this was indeed correct or if the delivery man or KFC had fleeced us. That's when they told us about the currency black market that was operational in Lebanon. That giant chicken bucket, fries and Pepsi had in fact cost all but $18. Oh! The relief – and confusion. How and why does the black-market money exchange operate? In time I learned how it worked, the effects of bad governance and how much the increasingly worthless Lebanese Pound was making living conditions in Lebanon so dire for many.

Our take-outs tasted a whole lot better though, knowing they weren't costing $250!

Julie

Harare, Zimbabwe (2004–2007)

BORN AND RAISED IN UGANDA, it had never occurred to me that I'd permanently leave my home town of Kampala, away from family, friends and my dear mum – that woman and I are joined at the hip. I just couldn't imagine living anywhere else. After graduating from University, I had my sights firmly set on building and developing a solid career in Uganda. I quickly landed a job in Corporate Banking, moved out of 'Hotel Mama' and started enjoying my monthly pay cheques as well as money from my side gig as a part-time model. I imagined I would eventually settle down with a tall, dark and handsome Itesot man (a native from Teso-land, my father's hometown), have a few kids (about five or ten; Itesot standard measurement for *a few*) and live happily ever after.

Well, that Itesot man never came to fruition but the latter part of happily ever after, I did get when I met this tall, dark (dark white that is) handsome French man with blue eyes. The click was instant and we began dating. There was a catch though, a glitch to our otherwise smooth dating journey. My 'date' only had about a year and a half left on his contract in Uganda before his definite move to another country. At the time, I decided to make the most of the time we had left together and part ways when the time came for him to leave. Well, it turned out *Monsieur* Blue Eyes was as much in love with me as I was with him and with charming persuasion, he asked me to move with him to his new work posting.

I took a (very tiny) step back, assessed what made me happy. Apart from this wonderful man, his cute accent and boyish humour, I always had a natural curiosity to travel and explore other cultures and this was a big opportunity to do that. So, I happily grasped the nettle, put in my resignation letter at my job and made a life-changing decision. I walked away from a place I called home, people I loved dearly, left behind all the comforts and the social network I'd known and strode into the unknown. That was July 2004. The rest is ... well, this book.

Harare, Zimbabwe became the 'lottery pick' for our first home away from home. Packed up and ready to go, I was eagerly awaiting details of our flight – you know: which airline, our check-in time, departure and arrival time. But my soon-to-be live-in boyfriend rather excitedly announced that we would instead be taking a long road trip. That meant we would be driving from Uganda, East Africa to Zimbabwe, Southern Africa. You see, for an urban girl like me – born and bred in the city – a long road trip was out of the question. Long road trips in Uganda meant bumpy, boring seven-hour journeys to my home village, punctuated with regular road-side stops to eat meat on sticks and roasted plantain. Not exactly my idea of fun (well, the meat on sticks and roast plantain is fun – the bumpy roads not). But ... did I mention that I was in love with this guy? Well, I was, so I cried uncle and gave in to the road trip.

Day 1: Kenya

Setting off in the wee hours of the morning, the ride from Kampala to Kenya was fairly smooth and uneventful. At the Uganda/Kenya border we seamlessly cleared border protocol and were about to go full pedal to the metal on the Kenyan roads when we were suddenly blocked off by two huge oil trucks, forcing us and other road users to a standstill. Unbeknown to us, on the other side of the trucks was an ongoing protest to release a Sudanese male who had been accused of, and arrested for eloping with another man's wife. Word was that unless he was set free, the trucks would stay put. After what seemed like an endless wait (one and half hours to be precise), the 'eloper' was released and welcomed like a hero by the onlookers and truck drivers. Feeling like a superhero in spandex, he employed a presidential wave of sorts, grinning widely to his many cheering 'supporters' and well-wishers standing by the roadside, waiting to receive him.

With the town superhero free, we were finally 'released' from the road block and we continued our trip. Remember those trips to my home village I mentioned earlier? They were being fully reincarnated on this particular road. This road was one of the worst I had come across. So bumpy I felt like my inner organs were dismantling.

Hours later, we arrived in Nakuru Town and on to a smoother road – with all organs intact. We took a break from driving when we made a stop in Naivasha. Here, we spent the night in a noisy inn with crowds in the lobby chatting and laughing so loud and deafening music playing throughout the night. My partner – a very light sleeper – tossed and turned all night. I, on the other hand, slept like a log, entertaining him with a few snores (or so he said). I'm sure that bumpy road helped rock me into a deep sleep. At the time anyway – still young and carefree – I could sleep anywhere and in any sleeping position, even in the middle of bombardments.

Day 2: Tanzania

Still knackered from that bad night's sleep, we got up the next day and carried on with the journey, after all we still had days of driving ahead before our final destination – and need I remind my boyfriend that this was his idea of travelling through Africa?

We drove through Nairobi and headed towards Namanga; the Kenya/Tanzania border which we also crossed hassle-free. After a quick stop for lunch, we drove right through a national park where, in the distance, we saw a giraffe in all its grace, elegance and majesty. A few hours of driving later, we made a stop for the night in a modest, quaint farm cottage up on a hill. It had cosy tents, a little swimming pool and a fireplace – the latter coming in handy because the night was rather chilly. Our warm, spacious tent was comfortable and a good reparation for that previous night in the noisy inn in Naivasha.

Day 3: Tanzania

We were in no rush whatsoever to hit the road the following morning so we took our time to absorb the charm of our little haven while it still lasted, before finally departing a little after 9am. Crossing Tanzania was full of interesting and exhilarating moments. It's a very large country and it took us a couple of days to cross it right through to the Zambia Border. The country has some of the most unique, varied and diverse landscapes that alternate unexpectedly. Along the way we encountered high plains, valleys, forests with magnificent baobab trees, game reserves, savannah landscapes and in the distance, a sneak peak of the majestic Mount Kilimanjaro ('the roof of Africa'). It takes your breath away.

Within a few hours, we were over 1500 metres high up in the mountains in a little charming city called Iringa. Located in the Southern Highlands of the country, it is known to be one of the coldest regions in Tanzania and this was the coldest I'd been in my life. Here, we settled for the night in a small hotel.

That night, I slept fully clothed like I was going into combat – socks, gloves, scarf – the only thing missing were combat boots. Curled up in the foetal position and covered with a heap of thick blankets, I couldn't see across the room. My partner on the other hand was sweating with a single blanket (remember, he's born in France, I'm born in Uganda. Anything below 20°C was labelled "freezing" for me at the time).

Day 4: Zambia

We covered 800 kilometres before finally arriving in Tunduma, the Tanzania/Zambia border. Zambia is known for its safari destinations but our drive towards Lusaka was rather monotonous, consisting of flat and dry terrains with red-coloured soil and a few scattered trees. There was not much variation whatsoever. The Tanzanian trip could have raised our expectations a bit too high where we had become accustomed to the ever-changing spectacle nature so generously presented us. Nevertheless, the road was smooth and fairly good. After several hours of driving, we realised there was not much habitation in the vicinity so we instinctively started looking out for our next stop for the night. We jumped with excitement when we came across some local people by the road side and asked them for directions to the nearest hotel. According to one gentleman, there was a 'tourist' hotel a few kilometres ahead (*thank God!*), which we easily found. Sapped and drained from the drive, we had a quick bite and settled into our room.

I mentioned earlier that I can sleep anywhere, through any noise or any discomfort, right? WRONG! I found out that I, too, have discomfort limitations. We walked into our room and before us was a single bed – and by single, I don't mean what you and I know as single. It was the kind of single bed that my

1m50 tall daughter would find small. Please keep in mind that I am 1.80 metres tall and my partner is over 1.90 metres tall. Sprawled out on this 'single' bed was a 'sinking' mattress (in the middle of the bed were some missing springs, hence the 'sinking' feeling).

Need I explain how that night went? Just in case you don't get the picture, I'll try to; With those missing springs, the dent in the mattress made it inevitable for one of us to roll on top of the other and, going with simple physics, that meant it was the lighter one of us – *moi*. In other words, I literally slept on top of my partner (no, not in that sense, you dirty minds!). To say it was uncomfortable is an understatement; we had body aches and pains all over and were walking like zombies the next morning. After a quick 'dry-clean', we hurriedly dashed out of that inn without looking back.

Just when we thought the worst was behind us that morning, we found out that our car wouldn't start. Yep. The car battery, *complètement* flat! *Not now, and not here,* I lamented, dreading the thought of another night in that sinking bed! Luckily it was a minor issue that got fixed easily and we sped off.

A tourist hotel my foot!

Day 5: Lusaka, Zambia

We arrived in Lusaka, yippee! And what better way to decompress than being warmly welcomed and hosted by my long-time girlfriend, my dear Pearl, a.k.a co-author of these tales, and her partner in their beautiful home in Lusaka. She, like me, was just starting out on the expat adventure and Zambia was her and her partner's first home together. We were excited for them as they were for us. She indulged us in a delicious home-cooked meal; perfumed rice with a chicken coconut sauce that awakened our taste buds that we had long lost from the dry bread and *whatever-we-can-find* food we had been consuming on the road. To crown off a pleasant day, we took a dip in their swimming pool to cool off and relax our aching bodies. Bliss! Our room had a warm cosy feel. We had almost forgotten how wonderful it was to sleep in a comfortable DOUBLE bed with warm fluffy covers and fresh lavender-scented linen.

We were in no rush to drive down to our final destination (Harare), so we extended our stay and enjoyed a couple of days basking in *royal* favour, relishing every moment. I was delightfully treated to a much-appreciated girlie spa day by Pearl. What a great period of repose it was! Bless her.

A couple of well-rested days later and we were ready to hit the road again.

Arrival in Harare, Zimbabwe

We said adieu to our hosts and were off to our final destination, Zimbabwe. The distance from Lusaka to Harare was surprisingly shorter than I had imagined – a smooth five and half hours' drive that led us to the beautiful city of Harare.

Zimbabwe's economy was, at that time, adversely affected by a super hyperinflation (more of that in subsequent chapters) that turned us into instant millionaires – Zimbabwean dollar millionaires that is. Given this economic situation, I had envisioned arriving in a rundown devastated country but the opposite was true, at least to my naked eye compared to my expectations.

We spent the first few weeks of our arrival in a beautifully decorated studio owned by a lovely elderly French couple. It felt like walking into a mini jungle with four walls. There was no doubt they were wildlife lovers because the studio's interior décor embraced patterns and textures inspired by the African Tropical Savanna; zebra rugs, cheetah cushion covers, a warm fluffy leopard blanket, and an assortment of crockery hand-painted with wild animals. While I loved the warmth and cosiness of the studio, the stuffed head of a dead Impala (*a real one!*) staring back at me was a décor step too far for me. That animal kept staring back at me. Creepy!

Despite the political and economic challenges that the country faced at the time, the people were friendly and pleasant. The experiences my partner and I had in Zimbabwe are like no other, as explained in later chapters.

Johannesburg, South Africa – "Jo'burg" (2007–2010)

BACK IN THE DAY, I always had South Africa on my travel bucket list. A friend who had earlier visited Cape Town had mentioned to me that it was one of the most beautiful cities she had been to. I had also read about and seen South Africa on various media platforms and it was – and still is – among the most developed countries on the African continent with so much to offer. So, you can imagine my euphoria when hubby came home with the news that our next posting was to Johannesburg, South Africa! Home for the next three years. My heart sang.

After a year of anticipation, we finally landed at OR Tambo International Airport in Johannesburg on a beautiful summer day. The drive from the airport to our short-stay apartment had me in awe of the beauty and wealth of the city. We snaked through tall skyscrapers, high-speed eight-lane highways and a generally well-developed infrastructure with modern facilities. Everything looked impeccable as we headed toward the city – but the spell was broken when we got to Alexandra; a shanty township in the Gauteng Province of Jo'burg. Full of densely packed shacks, it was such a contrasting image to the skyscrapers we had admired earlier. *Alex*, as it's commonly called, is one of the roughest townships in South Africa, with crime rates to match.

We finally arrived at the security entrance to our short-stay apartment. Before us was a high steel gate with a fortified concrete wall, high-tech security systems and armed security guards that made The San Quentin Prison in the USA seem tame in comparison. Paradoxically, this security was supposed to make us feel 'secure' but it instead left me terrified. This here was the first 'brief' on the extent of the high crime and insecurity we so often heard about in South Africa. We announced our presence through the intercom and after checks and verifications, the gates automatically slid open. We dropped our bags off in our temporary home, a tastefully furnished apartment with modern facilities.

South Africa was, to me, a mélange of emotions; from the most ecstatic to the lowest ebbs. We had a swell of a time but the security issues sometimes restricted our desire to fully enjoy our stay (details in chapter 2). Nonetheless, I have no regrets living in the country of my dreams. One checked off my bucket list.

Antananarivo, Madagascar – "Tana" (2013–2016)

I WAS THRILLED at the prospect of living on an island and to me, island life meant basking under the sun, taking dips in the ocean, walking bare feet on powdery sand, wearing a collier of flowers around your neck, drinking rum and cocktails all day and watching more sunsets than Netflix. Basically, living on 'Island time' in two bikinis and one dress. However, as I would later find out, there was none of that in Madagascar – except for the rum. In fact, my expectations (*fantasies rather*) were so far removed from reality because I needed to drive at least 10 hours (or the flight equivalent) before I could dip my feet in that powdery sand.

Prior to our arrival in Antananarivo, we had boarded our flight at Charles de Gaulle airport in Paris. The children, the husband and I quickly found our way to the departure gate heading to Antananarivo. Not knowing much about Madagascar (except through literature), I was curious and excited to discover this part of the world. In the departure lounge area were a group of Malagasy nuns. The majority of the passengers on board had Asian-like features; fair skin, straight or beautiful curly hair and others looked like myself; dark skinned with gorgeous kinky coarse hair. An interesting diversity in the people that originates from the country's history.

We landed at Ivato International airport and after what seemed like ages clearing immigration, we collected our luggage and headed for the tongue-twisting city of Antananarivo – also known as 'Tana'.

Time check: 7:30PM, the streets were empty. It felt like a ghost-city. Not one human soul around – there were souls roaming the streets all right; stray dogs, cats and the biggest rats I have ever seen – but no human souls. Had the humans missed the street party invitation? I later learned that many Malagasy people avoid walking outside their homes just after dark, probably for security reasons (or maybe they are simply too scared of those rats).

We noticed a number of homeless people sleeping on the

cold streets. Prior to our arrival, I had read about the prevalence of extreme poverty in the country but didn't expect to see so much misery. Seeing this was so disheartening and it slightly diminished the excitement I had had about the country. Fortunately, numerous projects and initiatives to support and provide shelter to the homeless exist although the situation still lingers.

We arrived at our new 'digs' – a gated compound with several houses. Ours was a semi-furnished house with enough basics to see us through the coming months before the shipping container with our personal effects arrived. The morning after our arrival, fresh from a well-rested night, we awoke to birds chirping, uninterrupted views of the green garden and a bright, beautiful sun shining in the clear sky. Prior to this move, we had been temporarily living back in France and had experienced an exceptionally cold winter that year, so waking up to a warm, sunny morning gladdened my heart. I was happy to be back in warmer climes.

Curious to discover our surroundings, we ventured out and were pleased to discover a more vibrant ambience on the streets; commerce, artisan markets (that I grew to love), alleys, green hills, rice paddies, traffic and narrow roads shared by cars, taxis, bicycles, pedestrians, rickshaws, and zebu-pulled carriages (zebu, commonly found in Madagascar is a breed of cattle with a humped back). It was an effervescent mixture of colour and charm, a hustle and bustle that felt like a city rising from the dead.

Madagascar has always been and still remains a country I am very fond of. Life was never boring and the three years we spent there went by so quickly. I nicknamed it 'smiling Madagascar' because of the beautiful smiles the people so readily offer.

Conakry, Guinea (2016–2020)

TRAVELLING TO WEST AFRICA, let alone living there, was another first for me. Apart from their strong French accents and character traits of a few of my West African friends (from Côte D'Ivoire, Benin and Senegal particularly), I knew very little about this part of Africa. I was intrigued to discover the cultural diversity, landscape and rich history this corner of Africa is so famous for. Guinea has a vast wealth of natural resources and mineral reserves, in fact, the country has the world's second largest known deposits of bauxite and produces 25 percent of the bauxite used in the world. I had developed an interest for artisan creativity while living in Madagascar and I greatly admired West Africa for their craftsmanship and creative skills. I had a desire to experience a taste of West African influences and traditions, like the unique mud architecture of Mali, the colourful bold prints of their vibrant wax fabrics and the magnificent pieces they created from them.

I truly believed I had developed a strong sense of adaptability after living in other countries – until we moved to Conakry (or ConaCRY as some liked to call it), the capital of Guinea.

We arrived at a time when the country was recovering from the Ebola outbreak of 2014 that had devastated an already struggling economy. In all fairness, we had read a bit about the country in advance and we hadn't exactly expected to be wowed, but nothing prepared us for our first impression.

Gridlocked traffic ushered us into the city under a downpour the day we landed into the country. Humidity was high but the piles of garbage littering the streets stood even higher.

Being the wet season, the rain had washed all the rubbish downhill and dumped it in mounds of waste and piles of plastic bags on the side of the main road. It was an overwhelming sight. Sadly, everybody who visited Conakry for the first time mentioned this as the first shocking impression of the city. In spite of that, there have since been numerous clean-up initiatives and programs, both private and government-funded, working towards a cleaner environment.

One of the things that stood out as I scanned the surroundings was the colourful clothing. All around us were women clad in wax prints, some with matching head wraps. Guinean women are strong and beautiful with a certain aura of confidence that cannot be missed. The drive to the hotel from the airport couldn't have been more than 20 Kilometres, but it took us an hour or so to arrive , with the driver manoeuvring his way around trying to avoid the large mud puddles decorating the road.

We made it to our hotel late in the evening, too exhausted and ready for bed. To our annoyance, the kids' beds didn't have bedsheets. It was a minor thing to fix, we thought, so I called reception to request for fresh bed sheets.

Désolé mais il n'y a pas de draps (Sorry but there are no bedsheets).

Quoi? I responded with disbelief. Apparently, the room in which the linen was kept was locked and the housekeeper had taken the key with her. I didn't know whether to laugh or cry or do both ... I chose to go with a tired laugh and *ConaCRY* later!

The first weeks of our stay were a challenge, for lack of a better word. Adjusting to the constant rains, the heavy traffic to and from the kid's school, the flooded roads, the humidity and the general hospitality was exhausting and dispiriting.

One weekend, we took the kids out to a newly launched ice

cream parlour located a few metres from our temporary residence. We politely said 'bonjour' to the lady at the counter but, with the blankest face, she stared back at us waiting for us to point at our choice of flavours. She didn't utter a single word except the price; no hello, no thank you, no goodbye. *Rien, nothing, nada, niente*! At that moment I really missed 'smiling Madagascar'. With time, we got accustomed to the expressionless faces and as I would later observe, behind those faces were warm people.

Disclaimer: not all Guineans wear serious faces. We met some very pleasant people but the majority, especially the ladies, didn't smile much. I guess they just didn't see any reason to smile if there was nothing to smile about.

During our stay in Guinea, we visited the neighbouring countries of Cote d'Ivoire, Senegal and Sierra Leone. Here we found out that the people smiled a lot more than Guineans. Could the smiles be correlated to tourism? After all, these countries attract larger tourist numbers compared to Guinea where tourism is minimal.

Every experience teaches us a thing or two and Guinea was for me a real journey of self-discovery and growth. The four years we spent there were the most significant years of my life as a mother, wife, friend and a small business owner. Guinea was one of those places you would either hate to love or love to hate. We were told by the *connaisseurs* (expats who had a bit of experience living in Conakry) that it's a country where "you cry when you arrive and cry when you have to leave".

Well, after four years, I can assure you, I didn't shed a single tear when we left. Living there was an enriching experience but four years was just about enough.

Moroni, Comoros Islands (2020–the Present)

YOU WILL HAVE TROUBLE spotting this tiny Island on the world map. It's one of those countries that the guide books sort of forgot about, it's no wonder some people have never heard about it.

Located in the Indian Ocean off the East African coast, the Union of the Comoros is an archipelago of three scattered small islands: Mohéli, Anjouan and Grande Comore (the largest of the three). It is a tropical island with tall coconut palms, mangrove trees, pristine white beaches with turquoise waters and volcanic mountains.

September 2020; we set off to the Comoros Islands via Paris (Charles De Gaulle Airport) and braced ourselves for a very long day after seeing the endless queue at the check-in stations. There were gigantic bags, TVs, and boxes spread all over at the check-in counters. At some point, I was stressed out wondering if the plane would be able to carry so much luggage and passengers. Most bags were over the recommended weight allowance and many travellers were being asked to take out some items or pay for the extra luggage. One lady opened her bags and in it was an entire pharmacy of medication (as I later learned, it was a challenge to find certain meds on the Island and if you did, they were costly). After two hours waiting in line, we finally made it to the aircraft and hours later, the plane landed in Moroni City, amidst a lot of clapping from some passengers. Seat belts were quickly unfastened and luggage pulled out from the overhead compartments. I noticed that the lady seated in the front row had occupied an entire cabin compartment. She literally had 2 large handbags, three plastic bags full of items and a huge winter jacket – left me wondering how the heck she was able to bypass check-in security. *No wonder we were unable to find any free space in the overhead compartments.*

We picked our bags and drove out of the airport towards the city. There was not much to see; on one side of the road was an abundance of untamed vegetation and forests, volcanic lava rocks and a number of unfinished structures built with stone and coral. On the other side was the sea in its magnificence, so calm and blue. Half asleep and half dizzy from a long tiring flight, I remember thinking, *at least the sea is closer to the city here than it was in Antananarivo.* Moroni is the capital and coastal town of the Grand Comore (the Island we lived on).

The architecture of most buildings in Moroni has Arab aesthetics, with several mosques scattered around the city. With a Muslim majority population, most Comorian women wear long dresses that cover their ankles, and scarfs over their heads. The dress code is not an obligation for foreigners but dressing decently is required to respect the locals. The inner city is really small. It took us only about an hour to navigate through the entire town.

The people are laid-back, relaxed (*typical islanders*) and always helpful. The island carried an air of serenity. I had no doubt that my family and I were in for a real experience.

Home is where the heart is – even if you can't remember which box you packed it in.

— ANON

2

FEEL AT HOME

SETTLING IN

When the words 'Settle' and 'Temporary' are put together in a sentence, it becomes a sort of oxymoron, because how can one fully settle in a place that is temporary? Do we ever really settle? After more than a decade of relocating from one country to another, we have always felt that the words 'settling in' are ... er ... unsettling.

And yet, that's what we and many other families do year in, year out. From military families that are stationed abroad to employees of the many corporate and international organisations that have to change residence every couple of years.

Relocations come in different 'shapes and sizes': In some home moves, one may be relocating from one city to another but will still be in the same country, speak the same language, have the same traditions and cultures they are used to. Other moves however require a change in residence address AND country altogether.

For some moves, you don't need to put in much effort in studying the country's customs and culture while for others, no amount of extensive research into the new culture will prepare you for what you experience once you are on the ground. The logistics may be similar in most moves, but in relocations to places that are so far away from home – places with a different culture, language and way of life – a 'Lonely Planets' travel guide just won't suffice. You will need to take on the many challenges and joys in a raw and vulnerable way.

We arrive in a new country, the kids get settled into new schools, the husbands into their new workplaces, the suitcases are all unpacked and VOILA – another home away from home! SO, NOW WHAT? This is when we need to hit the reset button and learn, unlearn and relearn all over again.

Here's a peek into how we discover, adjust, fit in, survive and ... settle in.

Julie
Zimbabwe

THERE WAS a certain sense of familiarity about Harare that gave me a warm fuzzy feeling, it was similar to my country Uganda in certain aspects. I swiftly blended in and didn't at any moment feel 'foreign'. I often received a regular 'Uribho' (a casual greeting in Shona; one of the main local dialects) from the locals while going about my day-to-day business.

When we arrived in Harare, we enjoyed two months of sunny weather before the glorious jacaranda season rolled in. Mid-September to end October is a season blooming with gorgeous jacarandas. The city is engulfed in their sweet-smelling scent with alleyways of fallen flowers that create a blue-purple carpet on the ground. There is a profound beauty in watching the sun's reflection peeking through the branches to kiss the layer of delicate fallen flowers. These sights and smells made me fall even deeper in love with this city. The jacaranda season seemingly brought out a mood that conveyed hope amidst the ongoing economic meltdown at the time.

What I was not prepared for though was the African winter. With an altitude of approximately 1500 metres above sea level, Harare's subtropical highland climate comes with a cool-dry season between May and August. For a girl who found temperatures under 20°Celsius freezing, this was definitely not the kind of weather I had signed up for. The temperatures dropped really low at night it felt like we were in Siberia (at least for me). Luckily, even though it was still chilly during the day, the sky remained blue and the sun did not hide its face from us, so we were able to get our cheeks warmed and trace our shadows.

At the time, Zimbabwe was experiencing one of the world's worst inflation and the economy was barely surviving. Back in 2000, the government had imposed a land reform program to seize white-owned farms. The unrest that followed, coupled with corruption, political instability, mismanagement and decline in exports caused an economic breakdown that severely devalued the Zimbabwean Dollar. As the economy and the currency continued to plummet, the need to supply money increased and the government decided to print million, then billion, then TRILLION-dollar bank notes. Zimbabwe was at the time the only place in the world with TRILLIONAIRES (eat your hearts out Jeff Bezos and Elon Musk).

Of course, the only glitch with being a Zimbabwean trillionaire was that the trillions were as worthless as a chocolate teapot. So worthless that it was common to find million-dollar notes thrown about on the street with no one bothering to pick them up. In 2008, the highest printed banknote was 100 Trillion Dollars! A trillion is a million million. Please take a moment and let that sink in! Confusing, right? 1 US dollar was equivalent to a staggering sum of ...

Z$2,621,984,228,675,650,147,435,579,309,984,228

Again, I'll give you a moment to try reading that out loud. This mega-inflation sparked foreign currency, fuel and severe food shortages and a thriving black market. The inflation was so ridiculously rapid that you'd pick up a product from a supermarket shelf and by the time you walked to the cashier counter to pay for it, the price would have changed already.

Changing foreign currency on the black market meant cheaper prices for services offered by Government-owned Corporations (who operated under the official rates). For instance, the price of a first-class ticket to the United Kingdom with Zimbabwe Airlines was approximately 100 US Dollars at the time. The aircrafts were a little outdated but they were fairly comfortable, respected aviation safety standards and the staff maintained a high level of professionalism. I used it a few times and I'm happy to report that we arrived alive every time.

Transporting money around called for a large travel bag, a small suitcase or a wheelbarrow. One summer season when my mum came to visit us in Harare, I took her grocery shopping. Meat was as scarce as butterflies at sea. So after someone informed us that meat had been spotted in one of the supermarkets, she and I quickly dashed to the store to buy some (we were not missing out on this meat opportunity, *no way José!)*. With me was a backpack and in it were large bundles of banknotes. At the cashier, I unzipped my backpack and pulled out four large blocks of billion-dollar bank notes and placed them on the counter to be weighed (*yes! there were so many bills in one block to be counted, so they were simply weighed*) and off we went with half a tray of eggs, a pint of milk, loaf of bread and a kilogram of sugar (the meat was already sold out, ha!). The shock on mum's face was priceless, I thought her eyes would pop out of her head. In 2008 the country reached its worst inflation point – one of the worst hyperinflation in history – and the government abandoned the Zimbabwean Dollar in favour of foreign currency.

One of the top priorities in every new country is finding a home. Our search was always based on different criteria such as distance to the kid's school and husband's workplace, security and so forth. This sometimes made finding something we collectively love a little challenging. Zimbabwe was exceptional however because it didn't take us long to find a house, there were a stream of beautiful homes on the market. The economic crisis at the time saw the Rhodesian farmers fleeing from or selling their farms before they could be seized by the

Zimbabwean government, leaving a saturated real estate market with exceptional villas on sale or for rent at ridiculously low rates.

When it came to job-searching, this was not exactly the place for me to go waving my resumé to potential employers because employability prospects were dire for everyone. The economic calamity had already left devastating consequences for its citizens with a significantly high unemployment rate. Consequently, I decided to give my marketing background a boost by enrolling in an online postgraduate course with the University of South Africa. Self-study requires a degree of discipline and time management, in the beginning, I found it quite challenging given that my study desk was a few metres away from a very cosy bed. In the end I did pass my exams. ;-)

I believe the soul of a culture and a country is found in its markets. I have always enjoyed experiencing the vibrancy and the organised chaos found in markets; it is something that remains part of my travel ritual. The contrasting colours of fresh foods, vegetables, spices and objects all tell stories of a place and its people, revealing life happening spontaneously before your eyes. There was a fair supply of local produce and a limited supply of imported (exotic) foods in Harare. My favourite was the little farmer's market located a few metres away from our home where I made regular trips to buy fresh fruits, salads and vegetables harvested from a farm located behind the shop. The local artisan markets in the city exhibited skilful artwork amongst which is the famous Shona Stone Sculpture; an art for which Zimbabwe is popularly known around the world. They create amazing sculptures that range from small-sized to two-metre artworks, all carved in stone.

Prior to the economic depression, Zimbabwe had a booming tourism sector with incredible wildlife species; moreover, it is one of the rare countries with the famous 'Big Five' (Lion,

Rhino, Leopard, Elephant and African Buffalo) and was named one of Africa's top places to go on safari. The Victoria falls (one of the seven natural wonders of the world) as well as Lake Kariba (the world's largest man-made lake reservoir) are also located in Zimbabwe. The tourism industry took a big punch from the recession and saw most touristic places closing while others survived by a thread.

I recall one weekend visit to 'The Great Zimbabwe' – a ruined city in the South of Zimbabwe. Best perk of this visit was that it was only hubby and I (and the staff of course) present for the entire two-day stay. One would think we had hired the entire place just for us – it was a strange feeling for such a monumental place.

Amidst these challenging times, there was a sense of solidarity amongst the people, after all, *we were in this together*. We enjoyed great company with friends and lived a harmonious time together. Zimbabweans are one of the most pleasant and amiable people I know.

South Africa

WITH AN ARRAY of accommodation options, house hunting in Johannesburg was a breeze. There were plenty of good homes, we were spoilt for choice. In spite of that, the main concern was finding a home that was 'secure' enough, given the high crime rates in the city. We eventually found a charming home in the suburbs of Sandton.

Like many homes in that area and other suburbs, the house was located in a boomed-off perimeter (or gated communities) with guarded entrances, CCTV surveillance and 24-hour security guards (armed to the teeth) who made regular security patrols around the neighbourhood. Regardless of all this 'security', residents didn't feel safe enough in these so-called 'protected' areas and further beefed up their own internal security with an additional perimeter wall and other measures.

Our home was a case in point. It was a stand-alone house in a boomed-off area with electric fencing on the perimeter wall, security cameras, burglar proofing on the doors and windows, exterior movement sensors, infrared detection beams that were turned on every night and two dogs that we kept indoors at night lest they got poisoned by intruders, as was often the case. We had panic buttons in all the rooms as well as inside the car – all to alert the security guards in case of an emergency. We loved our home but it felt like a war zone at times.

To bring my anxiety a notch down, I avoided the second page of the daily newspapers that often featured stories about muggings, car-jacks, rapes and murders that had happened the previous day. While driving in Jo'burg, one never stopped by the robots (a.k.a traffic lights) at night lest you get mugged or worse – shot at. You just had to push that pedal down right past the red light (with vigilance of course). With that said, it's absolutely NOT my intention to scare off potential visitors to South Africa. I know a number of people who've lived in South Africa for many years and have never been confronted with any insecurity issues. Crime is prevalent in most big cities in the world (and Johannesburg is not an exception). With caution, vigilance and divine protection, we spent three wonderful and peaceful years in Johannesburg. No regrets whatsoever!

Our move to South Africa got me setting a goal to find myself a decent job. So I took active steps to achieve that. I updated my CV and forwarded it to a few potential employers. I was invited to some interviews and after the fourth interview, it dawned on me that I had the right qualifications for the job positions I had applied for, the right skin colour but NOT the right nationality. South Africa had enforced a Black Economic Empowerment (BEE) Act – a government-implemented policy that was aimed at redressing the inequalities of Apartheid in order to enhance the economic participation of especially Black South African people. Therefore unless I had a super-power skill that no South African national (Black, White, Indian or Coloured) possessed, I was simply not a priority.

My hopes of finding work were halted, which meant I had lots of unproductive time on my hands, so I took another productive direction – I fell pregnant! My priorities took a 360º and my only preoccupation was putting my head down a sink all day, waiting to throw up for the billionth time with pregnancy morning sickness. In the ensuing months, I 'waddled' to Alliance Française for French classes. Nine months down the road, my beautiful baby boy was born. He filled our lives with an overflowing joy that is indescribable. He was my little blessing and a sun that shone after what seemed like endless grief (details in subsequent chapters).

Participating in community projects has always been an interest of mine so I actively sought out opportunities to engage in volunteer work. It was a great way to connect with my new community, to meet people and to contribute to the betterment of society, even in the tiniest of ways. I signed up to the 'Jo'burg Accueil' Association; a non-profit organisation that welcomes new French Nationals to South Africa and helps them integrate. Together with other members, we participated in various activities and one of my preferred activity was our weekly visits to the 'Mother Teresa Home' – an association that supported orphans, the sick and the poor. Thursday was the day we went over to assist the caretakers to tend to the newborns and 3-month old babies. We played with them, fed and bathed them before we put them to nap. They were the most adorable little munchkins but I must confess, I had a favourite; Terence was a happy chubby 3-month baby with a cheeky smile that would lighten up the grumpiest of people, I always looked forward to seeing him. I hope he is well and thriving.

Jo'burg is not only the heart of entertainment but South Africa's most diverse, progressive, energetic and most visited city in Africa. Entertainment options come in plenty with fun things to do for both kids and adults alike. A variety of restaurants, busy cafés, theme parks, cinemas, cultural events, historic and touristic sites, as well as a haven for foodies (like me) with all kinds of delicious exotic dishes that will make you fall head over heels in love with this city. We often attended theatrical performances and jazz nights, visited museums and enjoyed the famous South African braai (an Afrikaans word that means 'barbecue') with friends.

One such museum visits was to the 'Apartheid Museum' where my husband and I encountered a tiny glimpse of life under apartheid. On our arrival, we accessed the museum through separate entrances that are clearly marked for whites and non-whites (now done for tourism purposes only – don't call the race and equality brigade). Hubby walked through the entrance with the sign 'Whites only' and I through the 'Non-Whites' entrance. The Apartheid Museum chronicles everything there is to know about the rise and fall of the apartheid regime and is definitely worth a visit.

One of the most exhilarating events we experienced in Jozi (Jo'burg) was when South Africa hosted the 2010 FIFA World Cup. I vividly recall how festive and electric the atmosphere was. The ambiance was punctuated by the sounds of football commentators on large flat-screen TVs, staggering crowds in restaurants and bars excitedly cheering on the 'Bafana Bafana' (South Africa's National Soccer Team) coupled with the deafening sounds of vuvuzelas (brightly coloured plastic horns blown by sports fans to support a team) blown in all corners. Hosting the FIFA World Cup games was a major highlight for South Africa.

Nantes, France (2010–2013)

THE ULTIMATE TEST of raising two children under the age of two years was when we relocated from Johannesburg back to my husband's home country, France. Our son – my only child at the time, was about one year old. When we settled into France, I realised that in order to integrate better in this society, I needed to step up my French knowledge. So I enrolled at the University of Nantes for French courses and soon, my daily routine was to drop my son off at his nanny, go to French class and pick him up on the way back home. Half way through the semester, I started to feel weak and dizzy. A few medical check-ups later and we received exciting news that I was pregnant again! I dragged myself through the semester until my body and brain – knackered from morning sickness and constant fatigue – decided we had learnt enough French. Just enough to get me by.

In August of 2011, our daughter finally arrived. Another addition to our family that brought us immense joy. We were over the moon. As a new mum in a foreign country, the trajectory had changed drastically for me; from no children to having two babies in a space of two years, in Europe. Many who have had a similar experience will agree that a little more child-spacing would have been most preferable. Nonetheless, she was everything and more. In the early months of her arrival, our son had started Kindergarten. It was a small school about three minutes away from our home so I would walk him to school every day while pushing my two-month old baby girl in her pram.

As much as I loved being a mum, life became quite monotonous after several months. I craved mental stimulation outside the 'gaga', 'pupu', 'baba' baby conversations. So, when I got the opportunity to pursue a master's program at *Audéncia Ecole de Management*, I ceased it. The cherry on the cake was that it was taught in English. It was an incredibly valuable learning experience that introduced me to the business world and where I interacted with students from all over the world. But juggling an intensive study program, late night course works/reports, and tending to two very young children was overwhelming and pushed me to breaking point. My husband was of immense help but he too had work commitments and daily commutes to work.

I desperately needed some assistance and thankfully, my younger sister Elizabeth who was on a long school vacation in Uganda happily came over. Her presence was a balm to our souls. Not only was she an amazing *Tata* (aunt) to the little ones, she was great company too. I have lovely memories of the two of us in our kitchen chit chatting, laughing and dancing away with the kids to our local Ugandan music. We were even inspired to create our own break dance to a popular Ugandan song (ha!). We made apple tarts, delighted ourselves in *crêpes salées*, travelled around France, enjoyed our Sunday church fellowships, picnics and walks in the parks. She even squeezed in French classes at the language school to improve the art of *je ne sais quoi*. Besides my husband, having her as a support system was truly a blessing.

Our Daughter Goes Missing

Remember those morning drop-offs for my son to his school near our home? Well, our darling daughter, who was almost two years old, was cleverly mapping out the route we were taking. One warm summer afternoon in July, our precious daughter disappeared from our sight. That day, we had a house full of family members and we were preparing to drive off for a picnic in the park. Some were already outside waiting by the car and chatting away, others were packing up bites to eat downstairs and I was upstairs picking out the children's change of clothes.

The risk of having many 'responsible' people in the same house is the tendency for one adult to assume that the little one is with the other adult – big mistake! Just when we were all set and ready to jump into the car, we realised she was missing. We checked inside the house but could not find her. We called out her name, no response. Mere words cannot describe the wave of panic and the rollercoaster of emotions that were running through my mind as I frantically ran to our neighbours asking them if they had seen her in the vicinity. We yelled out her name hoping she would suddenly pop out of her 'hiding' spot and shout out *coucou* like she loved doing, but she was AWOL.

The first few minutes are the most crucial in finding a missing person so my husband immediately alerted the police. He was asked to prepare a picture of our daughter with a description of what she was wearing to be shared on the Missing Person's database. While the police were on their way over, some family members drove around the neighbourhood searching for her.

In the meantime, panic-stricken and tightly gripping my young son's hand, I looked everywhere; the small adjacent streets, the neighbourhood herb gardens, the little park behind our home; all the while praying, hoping and crying. My son looked up at me and sweetly asked,

"Maman, are you crying because my sister is lost?"

"Yes my love, but we are going to find her", I replied.

At this point, all our neighbours had joined in the search, desperately looking everywhere for her. Not knowing where else to look and my heart racing out of my chest, I was breathless with worry with every passing second. Then suddenly ... from a distance I heard one of our neighbours speak out the only words I so badly needed to hear; *Elle est là* (she is here).

Narrating this story still brings me to tears. I vividly remember every detail and I am getting goosebumps as I narrate this. When I heard the neighbour's words, I didn't look up. Instead, I fell to the ground, bowed my head and uttered *thank you, thank you, thank you* to the Almighty God. *Elle est là*! Those three words brought so much relief to my soul, my heart and my entire being. I looked up when she drew closer to me. There she was. My beautiful baby girl with her big brown eyes innocently staring at me. She didn't seem to comprehend what was happening or why my eyes were puffy and swollen from crying. I hugged her so tight, I didn't want to let her go. It was emotionally challenging to keep calm and not scare her but it was also important that she realised the gravity of the situation. With her tiny hands in mine, I gently touched her cheeks and delectably told her to never wander away alone again because it made Maman, Papa and many other people very very sad. I think she understood.

Turns out the neighbour found her in the playground of my son's school, totally unbothered and happily swinging and playing on the slides. *The innocence and fearlessness of a child*! She still maintains a fearless and daring character to this day. As long as she doesn't jump into a river full of crocodiles, we will continue to encourage and support her daring spirit. We immediately called and informed the police (who were already on the way over) that she had been found safe and sound. Phew! Those were the longest 7–10 minutes of our lives!

A little later in the day, when the mental and emotional distress had subsided, she mentioned seeing our neighbour's cat (which she adored) in the backyard. Our guess is she probably pursued the cat and when she lost sight of it, the only path she knew well was the one that led to my son's school, so she naturally continued in that direction. Some may criticise and throw stones at us for being 'irresponsible' parents but any parent who dearly loves their family would never intentionally let their child wander off alone (don't judge). I am so grateful to her guardian angels and for divine protection that was upon her.

Madagascar – "Mada"

UNLIKE THE TALL SKYSCRAPERS and modern streets of Johannesburg, the old town in the city of Antananarivo is far from a booming metropole. It has architecture that is a mélange of Southeast Asia, British and French influence. My real French-speaking/French-articulation journey began the day we moved to Madagascar. Prior to our move here, I had suffered a language block – I could comprehend French better than I could speak it. But moving and settling into this French-speaking country left me no choice but to up my game and start practising the French I had learned a few years earlier.

The house hunting experience in Antananarivo came with challenges. Most houses we viewed did not meet the essential requirements we sought: they were either far away from the kids' school, out of our budget, or required some renovation works done. Needless to say, I visited 25 houses before finally picking the very first one we had visited (*eye roll*). My husband *accusingly* thinks I do the same when I am shopping – *pff*.

Markets in 'Tana' had a delightful composition of colourful stalls with a bountiful supply of fresh food, textiles, semi-precious stones, jewellery, objects, and an evidently developed artisan industry that awoke in me an interest in handmade craft. Malagasy are amongst the most skilled artisans I know. What a marvel it was to discover their skilled workmanship; observing as they made magic with their hands and transformed any material – be it aluminium, horn, metal, raffia (a favourite), wood, or paper, etcetera – into beautiful pieces of handwork. My "Aha!" moment.

A year and a half after our relocation to Madagascar, I landed a part-time job at a Market Research Firm. It wasn't long before I discovered that the job didn't align with my expectations so after a year, I decided to quit and concentrate on community service. I derived greater fulfilment from carrying out part-time voluntary projects and being a mum.

Despite an abundance of diverse natural resources, Madagascar was (at the time) one of the world's poorest countries with an overwhelming number of homeless people scattered on the streets of Antananarivo. It was a saddening sight to witness and inevitable for anybody to feel compelled to offer some help; through donations or sparing time to support a cause. So, one particular News Year's Day I, together with my son and daughter (six and four years old at the time) decided to give back to the community. We prepared a big home-cooked meal, bought some refreshments and drove around the city making regular stops and offering a meal and a drink to each homeless person. My daughter, clearly moved by a baby girl with her mum on the street, whispered to me, "Maman, can we take the baby home with us and she can be my little sister?" I was lost for words but simply told her it wasn't as easy as it seemed.

As a member of 'Tana Accueil' Association, we participated in various community service activities, amongst which involved collecting and distributing donated clothes and basic necessities to displaced flood victims or selling items to raise funds for charities under the association 'France Bénévolat'. But none of those activities was more rewarding than when I became 'Teacher Julie'.

The Association was searching for an English teacher for children aged 12 to 14 years in one of the centres they supported. Well, I am not a qualified teacher but I got some English speaking skills so I naturally took up the challenge. On that first day, I made my way to the centre which was located in a slummy back street. I snaked through the slums and on arrival was warmly welcomed by the children. They wore the widest of smiles, you wouldn't know that most of them were without parents and many were homeless. They were enthusiastic, eager to learn and a fun class to teach.

Our stay in Madagascar was coming to an end. It was an emotional moment for the children, teachers and myself. That year spent as 'Teacher Julie' was a humbling and gratifying experience. Perhaps they didn't learn a lot from me; only numbers, colours, shapes, basic maths, grammar and a few games. I, on the other hand, learned a heck of a lot from them.

Madagascar is a large Island with significantly long distance commutes between the capital city – which is located inland, and the coast. Travelling in and around the country was largely with Air Madagascar – also known as *Air Peut-être* because of their abrupt and last-minute flight reschedules. You just never knew when or if the flight would finally take off;

could be hours or days. But once it did, the destination was always worth the wait.

The Island is a paradise of beaches, rainforests, an extraordinary wildlife and distinctive ecosystem. Amongst the array of beautiful natural wonders is the Avenue of baobabs and the 'Tsingy de Bemaraha' Stone Forest – the world's largest stone forest. 'Mada' is home to approximately 95 percent of reptiles, 89 percent of plant life and 92 percent of mammals that do not exist anywhere else on the planet. My family and I enjoyed travelling and discovering the Island and squeezed-in a few local tourism activities. One of them was our stay at the white sandy beach of Andilana Resort in Nosy Be (north-west of Madagascar). On the resort was a range of entertainment activities, themed events and excursions for children and adults to enjoy. Direct weekly flights from Italy meant there were a number of Italian tourists (approximately 90% of the visitors). Everybody on the resort, including the Malagasy staff spoke Italian and menus were written in Italian. It felt like a mini Italian city.

Exploring Madagascar was almost entirely pleasant for me, except for one not-so pleasant local tourism experience on Ile Sainte-Marie; an island off the east coast of Madagascar and one of the best places to spot whales. It was the perfect whale watching period and my family and I were looking forward to witnessing the spectacular whale-show. We boarded the boat in the early morning hours when the sea was calm. 10 minutes into the ride, the waves came in and I started to feel sea-sick. While the whales were putting on their spectacular appearance (spectacular it was, according to the others on the boat), I was busy feeling queasy and dizzy, face down throwing my breakfast right up into the water. Let's just say, no more whale watching for me.

For the average Black woman, hair is an essential topic that deserves a special segment in this chapter. Our hairstyles are so versatile – they can change faster than the weather. Our hair defies gravity like no other body part, has the ability to affect our mood and bonds us together through conversations. It doesn't even matter if it's grown naturally or 'sourced' (wink), our hair and hairstyles are a big part of our *hairitage* because we use hairstyles as personal expressions of who we are.

So, on the top five to-do things on my settling-in list in any new country is the task of finding a hair salon or hairdresser who will tend to my happy nappy hair. The hairstyles can sometimes be a 'miss' rather than a 'win'. One of such misses is when you find a hairdresser that tags and pulls on your hair right off the scalp like this one lady in Tana with iron hands that almost scalped me while braiding my hair. My head was so sore that night I literally slept as upright as a tower. Obviously that was the last time I saw her or used her services.

Over the years, my husband gained a skill; he became a bonafide expert in removing and carefully untangling my braids and weaves, when we lived in Europe (regular visits to hair salons in Europe is an expensive luxury). Bless him. :-) However, his 'duties' were relieved the day he mistakenly cut my hair as he took out my weave, leaving me with a bald spot. Another hair 'miss', ha !

Guinea

THE CLIMATE IN GUINEA is steaming hot and humid with heavy rains between June and September. It was almost intolerable to stay indoors without air conditioning every day, 24/7 throughout the year. Even with this extreme heat, I didn't miss the winter months of the preceding countries.

Despite its bumpy roads, littered streets, heavy traffic and developmental challenges, the city of Conakry remained a vibrant one. It looked chaotic and disorderly to the naked eye until you discovered what they called 'les secrets de Conakry'. These were places; hotels or private homes, located in the city suburbs that transported you to a totally different aesthetic of the city with ocean views and infinity pools identical to five-star hotels in the Maldives or Thailand. The contrast between the messy streets and the 'secrets de Conakry' seemed like you had boarded a flight to another part of the world altogether.

After five relocations in 11 years (at the time) I thought the task of finding a house couldn't get any more complicated – until we moved to Conakry. Almost all the houses on the market and on our criteria list were rundown, so much so that many required entire roof changes and replacements of plumbing and electrical systems replacements. Obviously, there were decent houses but they were all taken (actually always reserved way in advance). Frustrated from the futile search, we opted for a 'smaller' apartment by the ocean-side – small for a family of five. What I loved about it were the soothing sounds of waves crashing up against the brick wall and views of incredibly breath-taking golden sunsets.

Living close to the ocean had a catch though; waterfront homes trap moisture and humidity especially if they are not well ventilated . We were oblivious to this when we locked the entire apartment up (doors and windows) and traveled for our annual summer holidays. Bear in mind that we left in the middle of the rainy season. Upon our return, we were met with a musty apartment and a mould invasion caused by humidity. It was everywhere; on the furniture, in the wardrobes, on clothes, kitchen utensils, carpets, sofas and walls. It required days and a team to clean up and we were forced to discard items that were beyond repair. We learned our lesson. Two years later, we found a lovely ocean front home with a small swimming pool (which came in handy, given the constant heat) that was home for the last two years of our stay in Guinea. Like all 'good' houses at the time, we quickly 'reserved' it when we heard our good friends were relocating.

It dawned on me that searching and finding a job every three or four years in a new country was hopeless and time-consuming. When we moved to Guinea, I brought along my new-found interest for handmade products and the experiences I had collected from Madagascar. And here, a small handmade accessories business was born. This passion presented me the opportunity to organise numerous Popups and Expo-vente events. I thoroughly loved this phase of my life and even though challenging, I enjoyed being my own boss. It was a fulfilling experience that allowed me to develop my creativity as well as create opportunities for me to give back to society through supporting local Artisans and communities.

'Marché Madina' in Conakry is one of West Africa's largest markets with all tribes of merchandise; Chinese products, a wide range of fresh produce and colourful vibrant wax fabric. It is large, noisy and incredibly crowded with unending rows of shops and vendors. Much as I liked exploring the market, in the four years in Conakry, I still managed to get lost in the chaotic mazes of that gigantic market.

A 3-hour drive out of Conakry traffic and into the hinterland of Guinea led to magnificent landscapes, beautiful waterfalls surrounded by rainforests with the largest bamboos and a serenity that made you quickly forget the hustle and bustle you left behind in the city. Our local tourism was a visit to the mountainous region of the Fouta Djallon in the West, a tour of the late singer Miriam Makeba's former house and to *la chute du voile de la mariée* waterfall. The temperatures are cool and refreshing in this region, it was a good break from scorching hot Conakry.

Guinea offered the possibility for my family and I to discover neighbouring regions of Senegal, Côte D'Ivoire, Morocco and Sierra Leone. To my disappointment, we didn't get the opportunity to explore Burkina Faso and Mali, due to the ongoing political and security concerns.

When it came to my African hair tales, Conakry presented me with another big miss. One day, I walked into a hair salon, determined to cut my hair – well, shorter but not *short short.* For many people in Africa, cutting one's hair off is a no-no. Not many are 'brave' enough to even have the tips of their hair cut after a wash in the salon because many of us (read "I") spend decades trying to grow one or two inches of hair. Nevertheless, I was inspired to get a fresh new look (*did I already mention that our hair falls prey when we need a new look?*). I took a seat on the barber's swinging chair and explained to him how I wanted the cut. Either he misunderstood my instructions or he coughed and his hand somehow slipped but the *dude* literally mowed one side of my head to the scalp!! With this new haircut , I could not even have braids for a while, dammit!

During this wait for my 1-inch hair to grow back, I owned my new look with confidence and on some occasions I threw on a wig. Fortunately for me, wearing wigs was so habitual in Guinea so I was in good company. Guineans have absolutely no problem yanking their wigs right off their heads whenever and wherever the heck they feel like. Personally, I preferred to keep mine on in public.

COMORIAN PEOPLE are warm and welcoming. One thing I noticed throughout our stay is that this little charming island had absolutely no street beggars. Having lived in places where beggars loitered the streets day and night, this came as a surprise. My curiosity got the better of me and I asked Soilihi our driver why this was so. Family values take centre stage for Comorians. With communities so small, the population is a united cultural and social group consisting of a huge extended family structure, which means the majority of the people are in one way or another related (blood related). Since a family's reputation is of paramount importance, it brings shame to a family if one of their own is identified begging in the streets.

The islands are isolated with very little tourism activity, few (if any) entertainment avenues, and zero 'distractions' (read; shopping malls, cinemas, animated cafés, amusement parks or cultural events). The main Island is surrounded by the ocean, volcanic mountains and lush forests of untamed natural beauty making it a haven for nature and outdoor lovers. Activities are simple yet fun and adventurous; mainly nature walks and hikes up the volcanic mountains. A 40-minute drive from the city leads out to stunning beaches where you can enjoy sea activities such as snorkelling and canoeing. Unspoiled from mass tourism, the beaches were mostly secluded; it was not surprising to find yourself on one entirely on your own. In general, the drumbeat of the city was rather slow. Adjusting to island-time was a challenge for my family and I in the first couple of months, especially after *crazy and noisy Conakry*. But in time, we learned to appreciate the simple island life and it became a rewarding experience for our children who grew to appreciate nature and the outdoors.

We arrived in Moroni in 2020 with the COVID-19

pandemic and travel restrictions thereof still in full-blown mode. Over 95% of the limited selection of grocery goods available in the supermarkets was imported and came with hefty price tags. The major supermarkets on the island lacked basics like bread, sugar and milk, we had to wait weeks or up to a month before dairy products were flown in, even commodities like frozen chicken and meat were also imported. We learned to adapt and fashioned our meals from necessity around mostly fish, which we found in plenty on the Island.

On the brighter side, my preferred home was in Comoros. The house we chose to live in came with an annex that I transformed into a studio where I could pursue some personal projects. I loved *mon petit atelier*. It was my happy place, one where I cultivated and expressed my creativity. With minimal 'distractions', I focused on developing my business, had the time to write this book, enrolled in an online skincare course, signed up for boxing class (originally meant to motivate my son but I ended up liking it) and joined my daughter for tennis classes that I loved. I got hooked and enjoy tennis to this day. I happened to be the most productive in those years ... and yet I was the loneliest I had been.

While I was grateful for the opportunity and time presented to me to pursue the things I enjoyed, I often experienced waves of isolation (*a me-time overdose I guess*) creating a juxtaposition of emotions. As a family we supported and loved each other but I was yearning for good company beyond my nuclear family. There was not enough social stimulation and had some moments when I felt stuck on a small island – literally (*Chuck Noland, I know how you felt, haha*). Could I have been suffering from Island fever? I couldn't help but wonder what had happened to the cheerful woman who loved to host and share fun-filled moments? What happened to my motivation and zeal? Options for stimulation and inspiration were scarce and I felt like I was losing my *joie de vivre*.

Social interaction within our circles on the Island was rather limited at the time because of the curfews and restrictions imposed after the COVID-19 pandemic. I was dreaming of a retreat to a place that energised me; I yearned to share long hearty laughs, or plain silly moments with my girls and relive old memories BC (Before Covid), or see my mum and listen to her hilarious stories – and not through zoom *but face-à-face*. My inner child wanted to burst out.

I was not alone though; the pandemic had affected many lives in so many ways, some more devastating than others and we were all learning to live the 'new normal'. Fortunately, the period that had been characterised by disruption and volatile change began to gradually subside and we were able to gather up in groups again. Travel restrictions were slowly being lifted and we were able to get away and spend time with family and friends. One of my highlights thereafter was when my family and I paid a visit to my dear friend Aude and her family in Jo'burg, South Africa. You see, living in a place with limited facilities teaches you to appreciate even the smallest of things, especially those that others take for granted. I savoured the scents, the tastes and flavours of each mouthful, and every experience on this particular holiday. I particularly enjoyed our chats and laughs over long lunches and the evening we danced to throw-back music. :-) Those couple of weeks got me feeling rejuvenated and ready to conquer the world!

With time, I learned to be grateful for the calmer, balmer, tranquil life on the island and grew less fond of bigger cities (maybe it was an *age factor*). So even though we enjoyed travelling away for a while to catch a breather, I always looked forward to going back to the 'simple life' on the island, where I was closer to nature and filled my days with a blissful silence that kept me balanced. After all, people spend thousands of dollars for a chance to visit where I called home!

The other aspect I loved about this Island was its sense of security (a major contrast to South Africa). There was never a time I felt insecure. Although rare, there were a few petty thieves but in general, there is minimum crime in the country.

A 20-minute flight from Grand Comore Island (where we resided) brought you to Mohéli Island, the tiniest of the three islands with a little under 50,000 people. Amazingly this tiny Island has six even smaller Islands surrounding it. As you drive across the island, you certainly can't miss the lingering sweet delicate scent of Ylang Ylang flowers, vanilla and cloves in the air. The vegetation is wild, lush and abundant, looking like a setting from a scene of Jurassic park. A great place for eco-tourism, the Mohéli National Park with its marine, coastal and terrestrial areas, is on UNESCO's World Network of Biosphere Reserves. Hikes through the dense and almost impenetrable forests filled with tall majestic trees and green hills made you feel a bit like Indiana Jones on a mission. It is a hidden paradise with raw beauty, breathtaking coral reefs, splendid sunsets and Livingstone Bats (the world's second largest bats). Snorkelling and seeing the colourful fishes, manta rays, corals and sea turtles laying their eggs is a memorable moment my family and I hold.

Like its neighbouring islands (of Mauritius, Seychelles, Reunion Islands), the Comoros Islands has a lot to offer in terms of tourism but it remains undiscovered simply because of its under developed infrastructure. However, what is positively striking about this island is the effort put into preserving its nature. So, for those who prefer peaceful and quiet settings (away from crowds) in raw nature, this is the place!

I cannot stress enough how much I appreciated our stay in the Comoros and the other parts of the world we have lived in, for while there were many bumps and hurdles along the way, each one of these led me to the people, the places, the invaluable experiences and the important lessons I have learned. The biggest lesson I have learned from this expat life is, there is no good or bad place, there's only perception.

Pearl
Bangladesh

WE (WRONGLY) HAD such low expectations about moving to Bangladesh that I was still frigid with pure disinterest when we landed in Dhaka. So, it came as a shock to us when Dhaka turned out to be one of the smoothest settling-in experiences we've had while living abroad, albeit with a few – and quite expected – hiccups.

One of the first things we discovered in Dhaka were the Expat clubs; these are like private members' clubs with restaurants, sports facilities and many other services. They were oases in the busy Dhaka life. There was the British club, with exclusive membership only for British High Commission employees; the Dutch club whose full membership is for nationals of Dutch-speaking countries. The German club membership was for the German speakers and the Nordic club for people from ...? You guessed it ... those blond, blue-eyed Nordics. The International Club and BAGHA club catered for all other nationalities and the American club was for Americans as well as Diplomatic passport holders.

Once you had membership to any one of these clubs, you were allowed access to all of them except the use of facilities like swimming pools, tennis courts, and gyms which were strictly for full members. During the weekends and some weekdays, we spent hours in these clubs, socialising with a bunch of people, some of whom have become very dear friends. In the Dutch club was also a small Dutch school that gave part-time lessons to all Dutch-speaking children – another plus that meant our daughter, who was in an English-speaking school, could still have some Dutch lessons twice a week and keep up her Dutch vocabulary.

We had been briefed prior to our arrival in Dhaka that under NO circumstances were we to drive a vehicle ourselves. When we arrived in Dhaka, we fully understood why. The traffic and the absolutely loco, bananas, bonkers, manic, cracked, gaga, nutty way of driving in Dhaka is something one has to see to believe. It takes your breath away – but not in a good way (and for many road users, it unfortunately takes their breath away permanently).

We were advised to get a personal driver who could take us where we had to be during the day. Every evening, when the driver was back home, we had to use the cars and drivers from my husband's office. Please don't think this was a luxury – it was a necessity to keep us sane and alive on the streets of Dhaka. There were always two or three drivers on rotational night duty for the entire delegation and the system worked very well because all employees lived close to one another, so we car-pooled for pick-ups and drop-offs most evenings.

Public transport in Dhaka is – to state it mildly – a death trap. The local transport system consists of 'buses' that are just scraps of metal put together. This is the honest truth and I don't have any other way to describe them. It is a miracle that the buses never came undone while driving. The first time I saw one of these road death traps driving around, I thought it was part of a 'punk'd' joke being captured on camera for a TV programme, because surely a vehicle like this could not be permitted on the streets. But permitted it was. It was a metal box on four wheels with one or two lights in the front and none in the back (back lights? what for?) and one or no indicators. It stopped at a 'bus stop' (read 'middle of the road'). It was bursting at the seams with people inside and YET about twenty or more people were still jumping onto it as it started moving. They desperately clung onto windows, the roof and any other broken panels of the bus that they could clasp onto. I looked on in amazement. I thought public transport in Uganda was bad but it turns out Uganda operates limo services compared to Dhaka. Needless to say, I never attempted to jump onto one.

Similarly, the office advised us not to ride rickshaws and CNGs (aka Tuk Tuk, aka auto rickshaws) in Bangladesh. Rickshaws however have a charm and they are a national treasure in Bangladesh and quite frankly, they were a lot more tempting to try out than those buses, for a number of reasons; One, I felt that my stay in Dhaka had to be legitimised with a rickshaw ride. And two, they offered you more 'privacy', with a maximum of two people on the rickshaw. Getting on one meant a much quicker journey through the chock-a-block traffic and it was also a good way to support the rickshaw drivers. They are such weather-beaten souls who nonetheless have ready smiles for every customer, every time. They peddle for hours, meandering through traffic, up and down steep roads, chewing on their betel nut, their lean skinny bodies glistening from sweat and exhaustion.

They ride the rickshaws wearing these very thin, sarong-like garments called 'Lungi'. One part of the lungi is expertly tied around their waists while the remainder of the garment is rolled and passed through their legs before being tucked away in the small of the back or at the side of the waist. The 'outfit' barely (just barely) protects their modesty. I heard they go full commando under there (yes sir!). Obviously, I didn't personally check to confirm this. They may choose to wear a T-shirt but most of them go around bare chest. The rickshaws themselves are hand-painted in colourful, albeit kitsch art that is legendary in Dhaka; elaborate 'shapla' flowers and 2D portraits of local film stars – it truly is a sight to behold. I took my first rickshaw ride about a year after arriving in Dhaka when my dear friend Stella came to visit us from the United Kingdom and begged me to jump on one. After a night out at the Nordic club, we hopped on one that expertly dodged the potholes and quickly and safely brought us home at 2am. We had a wonderful time.

Mosquitoes and I go back a long way. Growing up in Uganda, I had dealt with the pesky little blood suckers since I was a baby. We had had many fights – mostly in the night. They had won many of our battles by putting me in hospital on numerous occasions with malaria. But I forgave them – until I moved to Dhaka. From the moment we landed in Dhaka, we immediately realised mosquitoes were going to be as annoying as a rash. This was exacerbated by the fact that our apartment was located next to Lake Banani with its stagnant, dirty water, which was mosquito breeding heaven. The first time we took the lift ('elevator' for your Americans) from our second-floor apartment was particularly memorable; as soon as the lift doors opened, the mozzies came swarming towards us like locusts. By the time we got to the ground floor and out of the lift, we were literally spitting and sneezing them out.

Dhaka mosquitoes are a lot more aggressive and a lot bigger than any I've encountered. Many of the well-documented methods of getting rid of mosquitoes were simply ineffective in Dhaka – lavender and peppermint oil just made the little gnats hungrier and like magnets, they just got stuck onto our skins, sucking on our blood, day in, day out. That idiom of trying to kill a fly with a sledgehammer almost became my reality because I was tempted to literally kill them with bazookas, cannonballs or whatever I could get my hands on. (I usually used something less dramatic though, like a tea towel that I would vigorously swat around until I was breathless).

Mosquito 'racquets' replaced my handbag for I carried a racquet everywhere. The sound it made while 'frying' those little pests was so satisfying. We also took measures to ensure there was as little interaction with them as possible by having fly screens on all our windows and doors at home. The little suckers still gave my daughter the dreaded Dengue Fever. (more on this in Chapter 4).

I remember the first time we travelled back to Belgium from Dhaka; It was quiet and mozzie-free but I was constantly and subconsciously waving away an imaginary mosquito with my hand. I just couldn't believe I wasn't hearing their buzzing sound. The silence was almost disturbing – you know, like a usually noisy toddler who suddenly goes silent when up to no good. I half expected the mozzies to be hiding behind me, watching me, waiting to pounce on me and go, "gotcha, haha".

No stay in Dhaka would be complete without a cruise down one of the many rivers dotted around Bangladesh. So, when Stella, my friend from England visited us in Dhaka, we decided to discover more of Bangladesh with a river cruise. For this, we booked a local tourist agency to take us on a guided tour. Early one morning, with a heavy hangover from the night before, she and I, together with my friend Shakila, were driven about an hour from downtown Dhaka to Demra Ghat which lies on the banks of the river Shitalakhya. There was a really steep walk from the car down to the boat and I nearly fell a few times (either from the steepness or the hangover or both, I don't remember). Through the stumbles and stares from the locals, we made it onto the boat. Nicely decked out with breakfast and a friendly crew, we were ready to go. As soon as the cruising started though, I fell asleep – only waking up when my friends screamed at the sighting of a dolphin in the water. Snacks and drinks were served in plenty throughout the cruise. The view along the river banks was not exactly Bora Bora but it was so relaxing. At some point we docked and got out to explore, walking to Jamdani village to visit the traditional Jamdani weaving community. The cruise took about 10 hours and it was worth every minute and cent.

About 90% of the total population of Bangladesh is Muslim, making it the third largest Muslim majority country in the world, after Indonesia and Pakistan. In spite of this, it is quite a secular society. While walking or moving around Dhaka, we were expected – and rightly so – to cover up a bit, after all, different cultures and religions have to be respected accordingly. We didn't exactly go around wearing Burkas but we were expected to, at best, put a simple scarf around the décolletage and not walk around in short clothing that exposed the skin. However, the heat in Dhaka is legendary and leaves you with no desire for any extra fabric on the body, apart from under garments. So, this was a bit restrictive (key word, 'a bit' because as I mentioned, we were not told to cover up from head to toe).

When inside the expat clubs, the 'scarf-around-the-decolletage' rules went out the window. You could freely prance around wearing your bikini or shorts. The majority of staff was Bangladeshi and still had to be respected in some way, but they really didn't bat an eyelid when they saw people in swimming trunks or bikinis.

The same rule applied to alcohol consumption. It is strictly forbidden for Bangladeshis to consume alcohol, whether one is Muslim or Christian. It is not sold in any public spaces like supermarkets and is only available in special duty-free warehouses. These warehouses were only accessible to diplomatic card-holders. The expat clubs, which don't fall under any particular embassy or diplomatic mission, didn't have access to these warehouses and were only able to buy alcohol through their diplomatic card-holding members. Having access to a good ol' cold beer or a nice glass of wine was another positive aspect in our settling-in process in Dhaka (disclaimer: we are not pie-eyed skunks who drink all the time).

In these expat clubs, we paid a monthly fee to be able to use all the club facilities like the swimming pool and tennis courts. Tennis was a huge part of networking in Dhaka. I had never held a tennis racket before but had always wanted to play. Before long, tennis became part of our weekend plans that usually involved going to the club late mornings, playing tennis, swimming, drinking shandies, playing more tennis, swimming some more and finally having all the kids together, giving them dinner, having them running around playing or watching movies in the club playroom while the adults socialised before heading back home. Enjoyable times in Dhaka.

In 2016, we had been living in Bangladesh for two years and had unexpectedly fallen in love with the world's least livable city (at the time). We loved it so much that we had agreed to an extension on my husband's work contract for one more year. June 2016 rolled in, schools closed for the summer and our daughter and I set off for our annual summer holidays, which we usually had in Europe or in Uganda, visiting family and friends. My husband stayed behind for work but planned to join us the following month after which we would travel back to Dhaka together in August. My daughter and I boarded a Turkish airlines flight very early one morning. The flight was half-empty and so we sprawled out and slept like we were in business class.

A few weeks later while in London, I was chatting to a friend when he asked me if I'd seen the news about Dhaka.

"What news?", I asked, confused.

He said he had seen a report on BBC about an attack in the city. A few minutes later, my husband called me and that's when I knew the details and scale of the attack and how devastating it was.

It happened in one of my favourite places in Dhaka – Holey Artisan Bakery. Located on a dead-end street in one of the expat neighbourhoods, Holey bakery was a meet-up place for so many expats and locals for playdates, coffees, bites or ice creams. The staff was always warm and friendly, the scorns and croissants sinfully buttery. It was another oasis in the busy Dhaka life – until 1 July 2016.

Five assailants armed with machetes, guns and crude bombs entered the bakery that day. They took everyone inside the bakery hostage. More than 12 hours later, Bangladesh security forces stormed the cafe and killed the assailants – but not before the goons murdered 22 people, including seven Japanese, nine Italians, an American, an Indian and two Bangladesh police officers. This horrible, senseless attack changed the face of the city and the lives of so many people. Many diplomatic missions and other international organisations, including my husband's work, quickly ordered the evacuation of families out of Dhaka. This meant my daughter and I couldn't return to Dhaka as planned. Our home in Belgium was unrented, so we were thankful that we didn't have to scramble to temporarily rent a house in Belgium. However, my husband – who had to finish the new work contract he had just signed – was still in Dhaka. A lot of what we loved was also still in Dhaka; stuff we travel with like our daughter's favourite dolls and clothes. Our daughter's school friends, our friends, our wonderful housekeeper, her children, our driver and his family were also in Dhaka. The ever-kind staff in the expat clubs who had become like family, were suddenly out of jobs because most of their employers had quickly left and businesses were shut. I cried for months, hurting from leaving and not saying goodbye. My heart still aches.

After a year of frequent travels back to Belgium to see us, my husband's contract extension in Dhaka was finally up. He then had the *enviable* task of packing up our belongings in the apartment – amidst disbelief over the number of lotions, soaps and creams I had stashed away.

"Seriously? Why would anyone need four lotions, six shower gels, five hair creams and all this nail polish", he asked.

Well, I always stocked up on goods from Europe lest I wouldn't be able to find them in the supermarkets in Dhaka. A case of FORO (fear of running out). Makes sense, no?

Bangladesh turned out to be one of the best work postings we've had, and having to leave so suddenly and unexpectedly broke my heart.

China

IN MOST OF THE COUNTRIES we live in, all employees are expected to speak some English. So, whilst it is always a challenge to move to a new country, communication was never an issue – until we moved to China.

Before our arrival in China, I was giddy with excitement about our move because what was not to like? It is a giant of a country with over 1.4 BILLION people (that's eight zeros after the '4') and a rich culture to match. It is also ubiquitous on the world stage with a thriving global economy – we all own at least one thing that is made in China, don't we?

In Belgium, I dashed to the nearest bookstore and bought a 'Chinese for Dummies' book, and – for good measure – added a DVD to my purchase. I needed to know a few basics of this lingo, like how to say 'hello', how to ask for directions, order for food, and so on. Two weeks (and one thousand tries at writing just one Chinese 'hanzi' character) later, I put the book and the DVD in my packed bags, satisfied that I could find my way around Beijing with these few words I'd learned, and off we went.

Hours after arriving in Beijing, I quickly got a rude awakening that the dummy book and DVD would not get me far. My first epic fail at attempting to communicate in Chinese was when I tried to chat (read 'show off') to the driver who had picked us up from the airport. I asked him something in Chinese but he couldn't understand what I was saying. This left me wondering if HE spoke any Chinese at all because I thought that I had a bit of the language basics in the bag. *Pfffffft,* I sighed with a hint of disdain, and rolled my eyes at him. Little did I know that in Chinese, word intonations and pronunciations are rule number 1; one word can be pronounced five different ways and have five different meanings. Goodness knows what I had said to that poor driver.

My next rude awakening came when I realised that our new housekeeper spoke not a single word in English. (as detailed in Chapter 1). So, as soon as I had unpacked all our belongings, arranged the furniture, put the mountain of trunks and suitcases away, figured out where our nearest supermarket was located, settled our oldest daughter in her new school, and discovered the neighbourhood a bit, I started hunting for a language school. I found one that was located about a kilometre from our home.

About two weeks after our arrival in China, we were able to use the very efficient taxi service called 'DiDi' which is China's version of 'Uber'. The greatest challenge was the fact that over 98% of the drivers (according to their own estimate) speak only Chinese. You can imagine my elation when I took a DiDi one time and the driver spoke English to me. It was like walking in a desert for weeks without water before you suddenly come across a lake. I screamed with pure happiness, asking if I could just hang onto him for the rest of the day. He was very amused.

Any newcomer to China has to contend with the wide use of the legendary chat and payment APP known as WeChat (*wēixin* in Chinese). It is basically like 'WhatsApp' or 'Telegram' but with a lot more functions. It is not only used for message sharing and making calls but also one of the most widely used forms of payment in China. It is as inescapable as learning Mandarin and it takes quite a while to get used to. The first thing anyone in China asks you is *ni you wēixin ma?* (do you have WeChat?). If you shake your head 'no', they will look at you like you have two heads and will ask you what planet you just landed from.

Downloading the APP was the first step. Once I opened my Chinese bank account, I linked it to my WeChat which then linked it to my DiDi, Mobike (bike sharing), AliPay (a big online payment platform which is not only operational in China but in many other countries worldwide), and many other APPs.

China is big on technology and the rate at which it is advancing is mind-blowing. In China, one only needs to carry a mobile phone around – no bag, no wallets, to have access to everything; payments, making calls, accessing memberships and numerous other services. Once you got the 'ang of the APPs, life became quite easy indeed.

Staying with the astronomical tech advances in China, it is

for this reason I believe that people are enslaved to their phones. They will aimlessly walk into you or bump you right off a sidewalk while they stare at their mobile phones. It is very common for two or more people to walk into a restaurant or café together and instead of eating and talking to each other, they stare at their mobile phones, quietly scrolling through messages, watching videos, buying things online, making payments – all without saying a single word to each other. It is quite amusing to watch.

We arrived in Beijing at the beginning of August. The weather was still warm and pleasant. Once we were able to use the bike sharing APP, we started exploring our Beijing neighbourhood on bikes, riding through many downtown markets and malls. Beijing is a city of around 23 million people (that's MORE THAN double the entire population of Belgium) and so there's certainly traffic to match that number but Beijing traffic was child's play compared to where our previous work posting in Dhaka.

One of the things I wasn't prepared for in Beijing was the amount of staring and photo-taking we got. Again, we had lived in Bangladesh where staring was like a recreational hobby for many people. In Dhaka we never ventured too far on foot, so the staring only happened when we went to touristic sights or to the markets. In Beijing however, we walked and rode bikes around the city quite a lot, so we noticed the staring a lot more. Many locals won't hesitate to ask you to pose for a photo with their grandfather while some won't even bother asking, they will just click away. I tried to tolerate it when it was done to me – I often grinned and bore it for the sake of culture but I drew a clear line when they tried to take photos of my children. I'd blocked them off immediately and in turn, I'd whip out my phone and try to take pictures of them myself –

giving them a taste of their own medicine. *Wǒ de xiǎo hái bù shì lái gěi nǐ pāi zhào de!*

The metro system in Beijing is a world class, state-of-the-art, superefficient transport system which is easy and very affordable to use. Before 2008, the public transport system signages and metro stops were all written in Mandarin (*han zi*). This was changed when Beijing hosted the 2008 Olympic games so that the visiting foreign athletes and spectators could easily find their way around Beijing. I was happy we had moved here after 2008. It was almost too easy finding your way around. We took the metro one weekend headed towards Tiān'ānmén Square and the Forbidden City, which was a 15-minutes-drive from our apartment. This place was *numero uno* on our must-visit places in China.

The metro was as dizzyingly congested as one would expect of a city like Beijing. We got off at Tiān'ānmén Square and tried to navigate through the massive crowds lining up to buy entry tickets to the palace. That didn't work. So, we wandered around outside the palace, ate ice cream and took hundreds of photo requests from hundreds of strangers, with some politely asking for our photos while others just walked right in front of us and proceeded to take selfies. We must be 'featured' in over a million photo albums in China. When the 'photoshoots' with strangers got a bit too much, we decided we would try to enter the Forbidden City another time and we headed back home. We didn't wait too long before trying again. This time though, we decided to go with a tour company that arranged everything from transportation to the entry tickets and lunch. It made things a lot easier.

Similarly, a few months after our arrival in China, we decided to visit Tianjin, a coastal metropolis of around 15 million people, situated about 30 minutes from Beijing when travelling by high-speed train. We tried to book our train tickets online but that didn't work. The online booking platform however showed there was a train to and from Tianjin every 30 minutes of every day of the week, starting from around 6am until late in the evening. So, we figured it would be OK to go to the station on the day we were travelling and simply buy the tickets there. Problem solved.

We arrived at the station and located the ticket machines. After several attempts at trying to purchase the tickets and thinking that the machines were probably not working, we eventually realised that tickets were sold out. Yep, every single seat on every single train, every 30 minutes of that day was booked. Still not wanting to believe that over 32 huge, long, trains running to Tianjin that day, with over I-don't-know-how-many seats, were all fully booked, we decided to make the long queue for the ticket counters. There, they confirmed to us that all tickets were indeed sold out that day. That is how busy the China transport system can get.

And don't get me started on trying to book a plane or flight when it's a national holiday in China, especially during the famous Chinese New Year holiday. Tickets are sold out months in advance. In the end, we booked a taxi that took us to Tianjin in two hours. We managed to bag return tickets on the train.

China is synonymous with manufacturing and trade and 'Made in China' products are ubiquitous. This was one of the reasons I was excited to be living in China. I'm not a shopaholic – although my husband will say otherwise – but who would not want a chance to grab some bargains in the numerous markets in China.

I expected to find a lot of goods in Beijing but I was still taken aback by the sheer number of markets and the availability of both goods and services in China. It is mind boggling. From the famous Silk and Pearl Markets in Beijing (they don't sell only Silk and Pearls) to Bairong Market, Panjiayuan Flea Market and Gaobeidian Furniture Street, you are truly spoiled for choice. There's an entire mall called Jinsong Glasses City that sells only eyewear. Here, you can get any shape, size, brand and colour of eye wear, with or without prescription, for as little as $10. It is insane. There are similar specialist malls selling anything from furniture to curtains, kitchenware and plenty of other things. I traversed these markets plenty of times with friends and I was still in awe every time I visited.

Oh, that latest Gucci, Fendi, Prada or Hermes bag, belt or shoes you've been admiring in the glossy magazines? They are all a fraction of the 'actual' price.

If walking through these markets leaves you out of breath, you can shop for the items online through the numerous online shopping sites, or through the merchandisers' WeChat accounts and have everything delivered to your door within hours or a day – including Sunday. One of the most famous e-commerce sites is called 'Taobao'. It is basically like eBay, only with a billion times more goods on offer. You can get anything and everything on Taobao. From pianos to earbuds, socks to cups, tweezers and scarves, shoes or sofas – anything. The downside to all his of course was my bank balance which suffered greatly while we were living in China.

When it came to food, I was in a culinary coma in Beijing but it wasn't with the Chinese food I was eagerly expecting to eat every day. It was instead food from other countries like Thailand and Japan. Chinese food, like most things Chinese, can be widely found around the world. I've always enjoyed a good Chinese meal in Europe. Part of the excitement about moving to China was that I would be able to eat Chinese food anytime, every day. I thought it would have the same taste as the one I was used to in Europe. But that isn't the case. First off, there is a dish for almost every region of China and the taste varies widely. In general, I found it spicier than I was used to.

Chinese also use pork and red meat in almost every dish they cook, and I happen to be severely allergic to red meat and pork so I steered well clear of most Chinese food. I once went to a 7/11 chain store near our apartment to buy some food. With the rudimentary Chinese I could speak at the time, I asked them about a dish that looked like chicken. I wanted to confirm that it was chicken and not pork – because the two meats can look quite similar yet I can die from eating one of them. The word 'pork' in Mandarin is *zhū ròu* and 'chicken' is *jī ròu*. I asked the lady at the cashier desk whether it was *jī ròu* to which she nodded, signifying to me that it was chicken. Back in the apartment, I luckily double-checked with my translation APP to see what kind of meat it was and it turned out to be pork. Clearly with my terrible pronunciation, she thought I was saying *zhū ròu*. I could have gone into an anaphylactic shock due to poor pronunciation. So, I only ate Chinese food when it was either prepared at home or when I was with a Chinese-speaking friend who was able to articulate and make sure nothing in the food had any red meat or pork.

There was a variety of restaurants in Beijing but one of our favourites was Flatwhite Cafe (Jianwai branch). Located next to our apartment building, it was not only convenient for me but it had the best burgers around. Best of all was the staff who knew what I wanted to eat or drink even before I knew what I wanted to eat or drink. I miss them.

The one cuisine that I unfortunately couldn't readily get in Beijing was my Ugandan 'matooke' – yes, even Taobao and all these markets couldn't magic this one up.

I am quite keen on Traditional Chinese Medicine (TCM). Back in Uganda, my maternal grandmother was an herbalist and although I didn't really grow up surrounded by herbal extracts, I truly believe in the power of plants and nature to heal most ailments. I found TCM very similar to African traditional herbs. When we arrived in China, I had a sore back. I found a TCM centre next to our apartment block where I received three sessions of a traditional massage and my back issue quickly became better. I also loved moxibustion treatments, Reiki healing treatments, cupping, sound healing and acupuncture, followed by cups of invigorating herbal teas.

Before we moved to China we were aware of the air quality status of China skies. So, I expected the very worst. However, I was surprised because, while there were still bad pollution days, it was nowhere near what I expected. I thought it would be like living in some weed-head's house – for shizzle, ma nizzle. Compared to Dhaka, this was as clean air as we could have hoped for. We still had the bad and really bad Air Quality index (AQi) days plus some crazy sand storms and these really put a damper on the day. I hated the face masks we had to wear on such days. In retrospect, post COVID-19 where masks have become our most important accessory, I think about how petulant I was to complain about wearing masks twice a year due to bad air quality days.

Although Dhaka is way more polluted than Beijing, I felt the effects of the pollution much more immediate in China than I did in Dhaka. On really bad days, I felt instant irritation in my throat, with a constant need to clear it more often (although I avoided spitting like the locals do). We always had air purifiers on in every room in the residence.

I thought I knew what a cold winter feels like – until we moved to Beijing. Winters in Beijing are chilling cold with average temps hitting –15°C. They are also bone-dry which means extremely dry, itchy skin, chapped lips, irritation coughs and the most annoying case of static shock. Humidity levels in Beijing are very low during winter so humidifiers run on full power 24/7.

While trying to settle into this giant metropolis, one thing I had to contend with was how difficult it was to make friends – at least at the very beginning. While there are thousands of expatriates in China, as well as the 1.4 billion Chinese themselves, I wasn't prepared for how lonely it felt at times. This was compounded by the fact that we lived downtown, far away from the Shunyi area which was the district in which our daughter's school was located and where most of her friends lived. In our previous work posting in Dhaka, we had made half of all our acquaintances through the school and we all lived close to one another. In Beijing, it became quite difficult to meet up because of the distance between downtown and Shunyi – about a 30-minute drive on a good day. With time, I met some incredible people and together we laughed, ate, partied, played tennis and visited so many places in and around China together.

China is one of the safest places in the world. Close Circuit TV monitors are dotted on every lamp post, traffic light, street corner, roof and door in Beijing and many other cities in China. While some may argue that this is an over-the-top way of monitoring citizens or an invasion of privacy, I argue otherwise. Given the sheer size of China and the number of people living there, this is a plausible system and it was one of the things I absolutely loved about living here. Crime, when and if it happened, is punished with the swiftest and toughest penalty. In many of China's cities, one can walk or ride a bike down the road at 3am, phone and bag in hand with absolutely no worry of being mugged.

Every *Laowai* (foreigner) in China is automatically baptised with a new name. My name (Pearl) suddenly became 'Zhen zhu' (珍珠) or the more formal version of it, 'Pò er' (珀尔). Not bad eh – my husband's Chinese name was slightly less 'sexy'.

Most 'Western' social media APPs are proscribed in China. Twitter, Facebook, Netflix, YouTube are all not welcome. To use them you need to bypass the pesky Chinese firewall by using a Virtual Private Network – aka VPN (I wasn't in Singapore or Japan when my location on Facebook indicated so. Now, you know). It is technically illegal to use VPNs, but so is spitting in China – people do it anyway.

Trying to connect to a VPN in China can leave even the most patient saint infuriated – it is often slow and you have to keep switching between several VPN connections before one eventually connects and stays connected. What's more infuriating is that once you do get connected, you cannot access Chinese APPs like WeChat. I had to constantly switch the VPN on and off in order to chat with friends in China as well as those outside of. Such a headache. I cannot count the number of frustrating days I had trying to speak with my family or friends on WhatsApp or trying to connect on social media and I failed. At some point I simply closed all my Western social media accounts, gave up calling using WhatsApp and chose to instead send voice recordings or speak to only people who had Teams, Zoom, Skype or FaceTime on their phones. My friends nicknamed me 'VPN' – a name I earned due to the number of times I complained to them about the infuriating VPN connection issues.

And Then COVID-19 Happened

We had been living in Beijing, China since 2017. In 2019 I got pregnant with our second child and travelled back to Belgium where in November of that year, I gave birth to our second daughter. A month after the birth, we got ready to travel back with our oldest daughter and her new, six-week old baby sister. On 3 January 2020, we landed back in Beijing, excited and ready to transition back to our normal life.

Mid-January, two weeks after our return to Beijing, whispers about a new SARS-like virus were doing the rounds in China. At first, we were told it was not contagious and that it could not be transmitted from one person to another through coughing. *Pheeew* – a huge sigh of relief. A week later though, when the famous Chinese New Year holiday rolled around, that relief quickly turned into fear because it was then announced that the virus was highly transmittable and was spreading at an alarming rate. China promptly went into full lockdown. Schools and businesses were temporarily closed. Many expats who had travelled outside China for the New Year holiday simply postponed their return to China and stayed where they were or travelled back to their home countries.

Amidst all this, I was still hopeful that it would be just a matter of weeks, maximum two months, before this virus would be brought under control and we would all go back to normal. So we held our breath and waited, inside our apartment, with an eight-week old baby and a 3rd grader. Reports about the virus were now dominating every news channel around the world with new information trickling in every hour about how the virus could be spread, the implications thereof and the rising number of infections in China.

As the nationwide lockdown continued, my husband's employer gave us the option of either travelling back to Belgium or to 'ride out the storm' in Beijing. We initially chose the latter because we had just gotten back to Beijing after being away for six months. We were also new parents and had a daughter who needed to rejoin normal school in Beijing after being home-schooled in Belgium for five months while I was pregnant. We just needed our normal life back. Leaving would destabilise us again, disrupt our routine yet again.

"No, we are staying", we said emphatically.

A few colleagues and friends were still in Beijing. We made it a point to call each other and get daily updates about the spread of the virus in the capital and elsewhere in China, and to check in on how we were all doing. However, as the days went by and the death count went up, those colleagues and friends started leaving Beijing and returning to their home countries. Almost every morning, I would wake up to a message from one of them that said, "We have managed to book a flight out before the borders close. We are out. Good luck!"

Seeing them go made me realise that we probably had to rethink our decision to stay in China. Our baby's second vaccination date was approaching but we couldn't imagine going to a hospital for the vaccine as each medical centre was taking extreme precautions with everyone – and when it comes to precautions, China does not pussy-foot around, everyone was presumed infected until proven otherwise. So, any access to a doctor would first require being greeted by hazmat-clad receptionists and doctors and being tested before getting any medical attention. All this for a simple vaccine.

Our families back home were also starting to panic. They asked us to get back to Europe pronto. After three weeks in our apartment – which seemed like months – we decided to return to Belgium *for a few weeks,* or so we thought. Once back in Belgium, we self-isolated at home for one week, even though this was not (yet) compulsory in Belgium.

The fear of, and uncalled for attacks and abuse against Asians in Europe during this period is well-documented. Any Asian-looking person was thought to be carrying the virus. In some circles, this extended to anyone who was coming from China, whether one was actually Asian or not. Some people did not want to meet us, even after we had been isolated in Beijing for three weeks and an additional week back in Belgium. I remember this one time when my daughter and I were going to the supermarket and she wanted to wear her Beijing school jacket. I asked her not to wear it because on the back of that jacket was the name of her school written in big bold Chinese letters. Such was the fear of COVID-19 in Europe that I thought if people saw her jacket, they would automatically think of China and run away from us.

After hunkering down at our home in Belgium, we thought the 'coast was clear'. We arranged for our baby to be baptised and invited a few family members and friends over to celebrate. Not long after this party, Europe became the virus's new epicentre and we went into our third lockdown in three months. Total bananas!

By March 2020, cases in China were dropping and the country was starting to get the virus spread under control so it closed all its borders to avoid any new spread and infections due to the rising number of cases in Europe. That meant we could not travel back to China – yet.

By July 2020, China was largely virus-free and everything was back to normal with schools and businesses back open but the situation in Europe and elsewhere was getting worse by the minute.

In September that year, seven months after we had arrived back in Belgium, we finally got approval and flight tickets to travel back to China. We took our (millionth) COVID-19 tests, packed up again and travelled back to China, ready for the mandatory two-week quarantine.

We arrived in Xi'an, a city located in the south of China and home to the Terracotta Warriors. We were scheduled to stay here for four days before continuing on to Beijing to complete the 14-day quarantine period. At the airport in Xi'an, we had numerous tests done before being driven to the government-designated quarantine hotel. We were given two very comfortable rooms, one opposite the other. All hotel room doors had alarms that would go off if the door was left ajar for more than five seconds. This was to prevent anyone going in and out of the rooms. Many families had been forced to quarantine separately (one parent with one child in the room) and were not allowed to go to each other's rooms for 14 days. However, we were exceptionally and luckily allowed to go in and out of our two rooms.

After four days in Xi'an, our COVID-19 test results came back negative and we were told we could travel onwards to Beijing. But this was not going to be any normal travel – we were still being treated as COVID-19 'suspects'.

The morning of the hotel check-out, PPE-clad officials came to our room and handed us our travel combat 'outfits' that consisted of medical gloves, hair nets, masks, googles, face shields and plastic covers for our shoes – the whole enchilada. Our poor baby, who thankfully didn't have to wear all this, was looking at us like we were aliens. Downstairs in the empty hotel lobby we, as well as our luggage, were sprayed soaking wet with disinfectant, just like we had been on arrival at the hotel. You would think that with all the disinfectant and all the negative tests we had already done, they would at least go easy on us. But nope, China was not taking any chances.

After our 'fumigation', we were loaded into an ambulance (yes, an ambulance) with all our luggage and with sirens blaring through traffic at more than 150 miles per hour, we arrived at Xi'an airport where we were whisked through a back security gate and straight onto the waiting A330 plane. The four of us plus an Embassy official were the only passengers on this massive plane.

The fact that there was no formal airport check-in meant

the belly of the plane would not be opened, so our luggage had to be put in the empty passenger seats for the two-hour journey to Beijing. Ground crew was under strict instructions not to touch any passenger's luggage (fumigated or not), especially those arriving from overseas or those still under government-imposed quarantine. This meant we had to unload all our suitcases from the ambulances – heavily laden with all the necessary supplies for quarantine like baby powder milk, diapers, wipes, baby food, cookies etcetera – carry them up the stairs and onto the plane, all by ourselves, ground crew just calmly looking on. Oh, and it was raining heavily that day.

Once we were on the plane, I jokingly asked the (hazmat-clad) cabin crew if we could at least sit in First or Business Class, seeing that the plane was empty. They politely said no! So off we went, feeling like VIPs on a private jet, albeit seated in cattle class and sweating in the PPE gear we were wearing. Two hours later, we disembarked in Beijing, were sprayed with disinfectant (yep, again), put on a bus and, with two police cars following us (in case we wanted to escape, you see) we were whisked through Beijing traffic to another government-designated hotel to continue with the rest of our quarantine. This time, we were given one large hotel suite so we all quarantined together. The view from our room was lacking but the hotel was great, the room very spacious, the food delicious and the staff spoke English unlike the staff in the hotel in Xi'an. We whiled away our quarantine days in the room with online classes for our oldest daughter, my husband working remotely and our nine-month old baby taking her first steps. Evenings were spent doing puzzles, playing 'UNO' and reading. Those ten days actually went by pretty fast and we enjoyed them much more than we had anticipated.

When we tested negative on day 14, we finally left the quarantine hotel and rejoined normal life in Beijing. I was so relieved to be back in China because while Europe and the rest of the world were in total lockdown, China was open for (internal) business. All restaurants, schools and other public places were back open but measures and precautions were still being taken to keep the country virus-free. The country's borders were also still closed off for non-essential visitors.

Lebanon

FOUR DAYS AFTER our arrival in Beirut, our COVID-19 test results came back negative and we were given the all clear to venture outside. Relief. We had survived yet another arduous process of COVID-19 tests and quarantines (albeit with shorter isolation periods than previous ones). We could finally head out of our fourth-floor apartment and get a taste – and test – of our new 'home'. The weather was gloriously sunny so I got our daughters ready and out we went. On the ground floor, I met the concierge and one of my husband's colleagues who warmly welcomed us to Lebanon and asked me where we were headed.

"For a walk", I said.

He told me not to go too far out as there was fighting on the streets.

Fighting? Why? Which fighting? Between who?

Turns out that days earlier, results of an inquiry into the devastating Beirut port explosion of August 2020 had come out. The outcome of the inquiry led to sectarian violence that broke out on the streets of Beirut. These militia street clashes left six people dead and many others injured. We were told not to head too far off and to come back inside as soon as possible.

We took a leisurely stroll a few metres away from the apartment and kept our ears and eyes open.

On this walk, I discovered that Beirut street sidewalks were no place for a baby stroller. First off, most of the roads have a steep incline to and from the sea shore, very close to where we lived. While the road steepness was not necessarily a bad thing – I took this as an opportunity to put in a good walk-out/work-out once in a while – pushing a pram up this steep incline was a sweaty affair. Added to this sweaty and bumpy walk was the fact that you'd have to dodge dog droppings littered on many of the streets. Some of the droppings had a human element to it – it was way too big to be coming out of a dog's anus. Whoever the doo-doo or anus belonged to was not the issue anyway. Once I overcame these pedestrian/sidewalk setbacks, I started discovering and enjoying the soul of this city through morning and afternoon strolls. It was immediately clear that this country had so much to offer – even amidst the economic chaos.

Our apartment was located a few minutes' walk from the Corniche (the seaside sidewalk of Avenue de Paris) and the Pigeon's Rock in Raouché (that place in Beirut with the iconic stone rock formations in the sea). These areas were always abuzz with traffic (that never stopped for pedestrians, even on marked crossings), joggers and people smoking shisha, eating and drinking in the many restaurants and cafés mapped out on the avenue.

About a 10-minute drive away, still along the seaside, was Beirut souks, a beautiful, commercial district with piazzas, all manners of restaurants and shops, including haute couture stores from Dolce Gabbana to Gucci, as well as a huge cinema. Not far from the souks and Zaitunah Bay were other equally vibrant neighbourhoods like the urban, upscale Saifi Village and Gemmayze. Walking and dining in these areas gave you a true sense of the beauty of Lebanon, with stairways dotted across the steep footpaths snaking through art shops, libraries and Saturday farmers' markets. It was magical.

As soon as both our daughters were settled in their new schools, I took a walk, happily wandering through our new neighbourhood of Hamra; a lively hub of Beirut with two major Universities – American University Beirut and Lebanese American University. I walked the busy Hamra and Bliss streets, exploring all the shops with imported clothes, shoes, bags and all manners of children's toys and games. We had grocery stores at almost every street corner with so many fresh fruits and vegetables. There was an electronics' shop every few hundred metres as well as a collection of restaurants, cafes, bars, gyms and money exchange bureaus. I had forgotten my laptop charger in Belgium but I quickly found one in one of the electronic shops. Not original but who cares, it worked.

Languages. Ha! Every time I learn a new language I start with the curse words because, it is %&$#@#%^ hard. Remember, as an English speaker, I'd just grappled with what is considered the most difficult language to learn – Mandarin. It has no Latin alphabet, it is tonal and frigging perplexing. And yet, here I was again, having to learn yet another non-Latin alphabetic language, considered the SECOND most difficult language to learn, with the same weird-looking characters and tones. The dickens!!! If I had had to learn all these languages twenty years ago I would have happily done so – brain was still fresh, no kids yet, enough sleep in the night (except for weekends) ... But now? This was hard.

Lebanon has three official languages; Arabic, French and English, with Arabic being the most commonly spoken among Lebanese. I was willing to give it a try but I found so many complications with it. First, Arabic has so many dialects. It is classified by region or country. The Arabic in Lebanon will vary from that spoken in Saudi Arabia or Syria. Secondly, they write from right to left – that alone is so confusing. Third, when they do use the Latin alphabet, they exclude most of the vowels in words, replacing them at times with numbers, *whch mk3s rdng v3ry dffclt.*

With this in mind, I set my priorities in line; what language was more beneficial for me to learn now? Turns out French was – given that Belgium, the tiny little European country we call 'home', also has three official languages and French is one of them. So, within three weeks of arriving in Lebanon, I was sitting down for a French assessment exam at the University of Saint Joseph. With time, I did make a small effort with Arabic but not enough to get me through a 10-minute conversation with a native speaker.

Power cuts were paralysing this vibrant country. Prior to moving here, we had been briefed about this – it was also all over the world news. The outages were caused by a shortage of fuel due to the worsening political situation in the country at the time. At one point, Lebanon's entire national power grid went offline for 24 hours. Fuel-run generators were the only choice – that is, if those generators even had fuel. This was quickly becoming a humanitarian crisis when places like hospitals were running out of fuel for their generators. By the time we arrived in the country, Lebanon had managed to work out a deal with Iraq for some fuel, temporarily fixing the problem for the larger population. In our apartment building, the power cuts were between 2pm and 4pm during the day and from 2am until 5am in the night. This was an alternation between the electricity generator and the national power grid – I didn't know which was running when, I just cared that there was any electricity at all. Not every building had this 'good' supply of electricity which, given the general situation, was far much better than other residences and businesses, many of whom were out of power for up to eight hours a day.

Walking on the streets, I was constantly dodging some angrily vibrating generators stationed outside shops and restaurants, powering on businesses and making a heck of noise and fumes. In time I learned all about electricity rationing; when to switch what electric appliance on according to the amperage that was allowed at the time, etcetera.

What Beirut lacks in public spaces like parks, it makes up for with the number of gyms, yoga studios and swimming pools. On one of my neighbourhood 'recon' walks, I came across a gym and on a whim, I signed up for a six-months membership. Given that I've never been a gym bunny and I had not a single clue on how to use most of the machines, it was a rather impulsive sign. They were on a massive promotional discount and they threw in a personal trainer for the price so I took full advantage. The work-outs came in handy because I often had to walk up and down five flights of stairs when my apartment building elevator was 'incapacitated' by the constant city power cuts. My muscles were getting a good workout for the very first time.

Beirutis are big on fashion; it is like a patriotic duty to always look smart. Designers and all major high street shops are dotted all over the numerous malls in Lebanon even amidst the economic crisis at the time. Shopping in such stores though – for even the cheapest item – meant carrying a bag full of cash because of the devalued Lebanese Pound. Foreign credit and debit cards were not allowed anywhere at the time. Needless to say, I limited my shopping to essentials like groceries.

When it comes to food, Lebanon satisfies all kinds of taste buds. With an eclectic mix of Mediterranean and international cuisines, I was in a food coma here. We couldn't get enough of their *Za'atar, Haloumi, Labneh, Tawouk and Hummus* (Oh, the famous *Hummus*). Other 'more Western' foods like sandwiches, juicy burgers, seafood and Asia cuisine were also readily available in the many restaurants around the city.

From quaint guest houses – many of them family-owned – to 5-star hotels, Beirut has it all. Civil wars and the devastating Beirut port explosion in August 2020 have done their fair share of damage to some architecture in the city, but there are still many gems of buildings, galleries and museums in this resilient country. Beirut neighbourhoods such as Gemmayze and Mar Mikhael offer eclectic trendy shops, markets, stores, pubs and restaurants.

Following government failure, large-scale protests and the COVID-19 pandemic, the Lebanese economy and the Lebanese Pound (Lira) was in free fall. When we arrived in Lebanon, it was tethering on civil war (to be fair, this civil war mood seems ever present in Lebanon with constant strikes and protests). A lot was at stake, especially the economy. Their currency had lost over 90% of its value and had been steadily hitting new lows on the black market. In September 2021 it was over 21,000LL against the US dollar on the black market. By early January 2022, it was at 30,000LL. Inflation and prices of goods skyrocketed and people became so despondent and disillusioned with their once thriving country.

While some people remained patriotic and defiant to the hardships, many were leaving Lebanon for greener pastures. Professionals like doctors were relocating to other countries in the Middle East and the West for a heftier pay cheque. On many occasions, people asked us why the heck we had come to Lebanon. People faced hard decisions on whether to stay or flee Lebanon and many families were split up, with one parent choosing to leave the country for a better pay cheque while the children and the other parent stayed behind.

If there's one thing Lebanese have in common, it's their love for a good party. We arrived at a time when COVID-19 infections were largely under control. Many of the places that had survived the hard-hit economy were in full swing, opening until late in the night. If you are wondering how, amidst an economic crisis, they were able to afford going out every evening or dressing up to the nines, well, Lebanese expats send alooot of dosh back home. Even though the economic crisis had severely affected these remittances, with the amount falling from over 8 billion US dollars in 2011 to only 2 billion US dollars in 2020, there was apparently still enough dosh for fun-filled nights out on the tiles.

Exploring Lebanon was one of the things I was most excited about. This Middle Eastern gem is famed for its historical towns and cities like Baalbek, Jbeil (Byblos), Batroun, Tripoli (not the one in Libya), Tyre and so many others. Venturing outside Beirut was so easy. An hour north (two, if you step on the brakes once in a while) and you'd be in Batroun. Byblos (a UNESCO world heritage town) is less than one hour away while Tripoli, Lebanon's second largest city, was only two hours away which meant one could easily fit three towns in a day's itinerary and still be back to Beirut in time for a long strong drink and party. For a small country like Lebanon, it sure packs a lot of beauty and adventure so we spent many weekends travelling outside Beirut, exploring the many cultural and historic towns.

Getting around Beirut by car seems easier than we had been led to believe – certainly easier than Dhaka and Beijing traffic. We had been advised to get a car in Beirut but when we arrived here, we realised that taxis were plenty and easily accessible. They are at every street corner, constantly on the look-out for customers and will (abruptly) stop anytime, anywhere on the street to pick up one. For better security and due to my non-existent Arabic, I used 'Uber' or 'ALLO Taxi'. They were very efficient and affordable and most of the drivers spoke English.

Many drivers in Beirut are fast, reckless and furious. They drive the wrong way, cut you off, double (or triple) park, drive while texting, chatting or smoking (weed I suppose?) and if you call them out, they will describe your (or worse still, you mum or dad's) nether regions and other body parts in the crudest way possible (my taxi drivers translated the Arabic words for me). Mind you, most people carry guns in Lebanon so, at times, I've been afraid of where the traffic curse words may lead to when I am sitting in a taxi and witnessing these exchanges. The Wild Wild West – Middle Eastern style. And don't get me started on the mopeds/motorcycles – loud, annoying machines waltzing around and causing road accidents. Even with such traffic scenes, I have never seen more than two traffic officers on the road, which is really sad – economic hardships I suppose. Still, the insane Beirut traffic is nothing compared to Dhaka – although Dhaka drivers are a lot calmer.

What (pleasantly) surprised me was how convenient and efficient online shopping is in Beirut. I barely went to a supermarket because everything I needed could be delivered to my doorstep within a few minutes. It was so fast it made China online delivery capabilities pale in comparison. We had 'Nok-Nok' and 'InstaShop' for every household supply, as well as APPs for the big supermarkets like 'Carrefour' and 'Spinneys'. We had 'Zamato' and 'Toters' for food delivery and have I mentioned how delicious Lebanese food is? On top of the online shopping, the streets were littered with all manners of shops; from electronics to grocery stores, all a short walking distance away.

Lebanese are very welcoming people. This was immediately evident as soon as we arrived in Beirut. From people offering to help with our luggage at the airport to strangers stopping on the streets just to say hello to you or help you when you have a question. Within a few weeks of arrival, I was very much at home here. It felt like I had known the corner barber, the grocery shop guys, the electronics shop owner near my apartment and the gentleman in the shop full of antique Barbie dolls, for years. I would always stop and say a *Marhaba* and make small talk before heading off to wherever I was going.

Unexpected kindness is the most powerful, least costly, and most underrated agent of human change.

— BOB KERREY

3
THE OTHER WOMAN
OUR CARETAKERS

As Africans, we are unabashedly 'spoilt' by having housekeepers at home. One's financial status has nothing to do with the ability to employ one. Oftentimes, even the housekeepers hire their own housekeepers.

Growing up, these housekeepers were part of our family fabric, with many staying on in the family for years before going off to marry or into retirement. Whatever we did, they were without question included; day trips to the beach, family parties, they were with us. Even with a housekeeper around, we still had to make our own beds, help with chores like washing and ironing clothes as well as cooking. We have always seen any house help as a valued extension of the family and not the ultimate luxury to have. We never loaf around just because we have someone helping us.

On missions abroad, having a housekeeper is one of the 'perks' that come with the relocations, and who are we to complain about that? Domestic help can range from a housekeeper to a gardener, a driver or a security guard. If you fall in the 2% of 'Hollywood-star-ish' expats (not naming names), you might even throw in a 24/7 fitness coach, a chef or an in-house nutritionist and masseuse.

Many of you may wonder why an (often jobless) expat wife would need house help, and that's a valid question. However, the role of housekeeping staff is a significant and valued one for both parties, in more ways than one:

1. Domestic work plays a significant role in the employment sector. It is a source of income for the housekeeping staff which enables them to educate and feed their families hence contributing to economic growth.
2. Some expat spouses have obligations that require regular hosting (official or private) which, with house help, enables them to concentrate on the aspects of organising and entertaining the guests without being overwhelmed with chores.
3. A clean environment (thanks to housekeepers) enables you to be more productive and maximise your day to take care of more important issues like your children's schooling and activities as well as taking care of the 'expat' himself (a.k.a. husband).

Having a housekeeper is an individual choice and we know a few people in the expat community who took the decision not to employ house help. For those that chose to have one, there are clear terms of employment for domestic workers. They are paid well, they get annual leave and additional allowances. They are the first people we learn from about the new country we find ourselves in, they are well versed with the day-to-day lives of local living and know all the nooks and corners that you won't find on an expat 'to-visit' map.

Together with our housekeepers, we have been a team.

They are highly valued members of our lives who have helped raise our children and made our households the comfortable temporary homes they are. They have also been privy to some personal and intimate discussions in the family – for this, we have bribed them for their silence. ;-)

Pearl
Zambia

MY THEN BOYFRIEND (now husband) travelled to Lusaka, Zambia a month before I did, so he met our housekeeper before I did. He said good – but not glowing – things about her. Considering he only saw her for two minutes each morning before he rushed off to work, and a split second in the afternoon before she went home, there was nothing much for him to report on.

When I finally joined him in Lusaka, I met her. Helen is the one exception in this otherwise wonderful experience we've had with housekeeping 'aunties' during our work postings abroad. I believe that meeting my husband before meeting me gave her the impression that she was going to work for a bachelor and so she may have been disappointed to learn that a woman would be arriving in the house. When I finally met her, she seemed unhappy, grumpy, grumbling and gloomy. Long story short she didn't last long with us. My husband's work, which employed her directly, terminated her contract because they too had not been happy with her for a while. A few weeks after her termination, she attempted to enter the premises, unaware that we had already changed the locks. She mouthed off some incoherent rants and threats before she was asked to leave the gate and luckily, we never saw her again.

Next came an absolute gem of a woman called Doreen. She, like many Zambians, was a warm, kind soul. We immediately loved her. She had one caveat for coming to work for us. She had a small baby she needed to bring to work every day. No problem for me. I didn't have children at the time but I wanted them in the future and so her baby gave me some good practice. She was so diligent and kind and having her baby around didn't stop her fulfilling her duties.

In addition to Doreen, we had a gardener. We didn't hire him though (no, we don't live THAT luxuriously); he was a package deal that 'came' with the house and was paid for by the landlord. He worked in both our garden and at the landlord's house which was right behind our rented house. He helped maintain the garden as well as keep our small swimming pool clean. He was also responsible for running or servicing the power generator when needed (and boy did we need that generator – there were so many power outages in Lusaka at that time).

Bangladesh

ON ARRIVAL IN DHAKA, bleary-eyed and tired from a long-haul flight, I was tempted to crawl into bed and sleep off the exhaustion. But I was looking at a mountain of suitcases that needed unpacking and sorting. You see, I have a mild case of obsessive compulsive disorder (OCD) when it comes to packing, unpacking and arranging stuff during our travels; be it for long term moves abroad or short holidays, I can't settle when luggage is still in the suitcases. As soon as we arrive, everything has to be unpacked and put in the right place; it doesn't matter whether it's in the middle of the night or if the birds are chirping at dawn. The socks have to go in drawers, jackets, shirts and dresses on clothes hangers, T-shirts and undergarments have to be folded away nicely, shoes and laundry put away. So, this is the first thing I did on arrival in our apartment in Dhaka while my husband and daughter sensibly went off to bed to sleep off the jet lag.

About half an hour later, there was a knock on the door and I opened it to two ladies. One introduced herself as the head of housekeeping. She then introduced the lady with her as our new housekeeper, a.k.a 'Aya'. Suchitra is the absolute definition of warm and kind. I immediately liked her. She dove right into helping me unpack, arranging clothes and bedding for our daughter's room – which is always a priority. It didn't take long for her and our oldest daughter to become thick as thieves.

We lived on a narrow dead-end street and the school bus was unable to drive into the street. That meant I had to walk about 200 metres to the main road to drop off and pick up our daughter from the bus. Now, I did mention in previous chapters that one of the biggest pastime hobbies for most Bangladeshis is the art of STARING. This short walk, all 200 metres from our apartment entry gate to the main road, was full of hundreds of pairs of staring eyes. They were friendly stares but nonetheless, stares. At first, I tried to ignore them but after a while, I was at my wits end dreading that 200-metre journey. Suchitra kindly offered to go pick up our daughter from the bus, something she didn't have to do. After a while, due to security concerns detailed in chapter 5, we stopped using the school bus and I picked up our daughter from school with our driver.

Suchitra also earned extra money babysitting our daughter while we were out for occasional dinners or drinks. She usually brought her daughter along who happily played with our daughter until they both went to bed.

She mentioned one day that she wanted to learn how to cook 'Western' dishes. Now, I'm no Nigella Lawson in the kitchen (my poor husband can attest to that), but I gave her a few lessons on preparing some simple food like quiches, mini pizzas and some meats. Before long, she was gladly helping me with lunch preparations. Nothing was too much for her. With our unexpected departure from Dhaka almost three years later, she is one of the people I missed the most. We are still in touch to this day.

China

ARRIVING IN BEIJING after a 12-hour flight from Belgium, I was pretty excited that we would be calling this ginormous metropole 'home' for the next few years and not even the long immigration queue at the airport nor the almost 2-hour car ride from the airport to our apartment was going to dampen my happy mood. With over 14 suitcases, we arrived at our new apartment and while my husband and daughter fell asleep soon after (as they do), I dived right into my OCD tendencies of unpacking. A few hours later, it was time to meet our new housekeeper. This is someone I spend more time with during the day than my own husband and children, so I am always eager to know more about them and make them feel like part of the family.

Brought in by Kat, who was the head of housekeeping, Ruo Mei Ayi (Auntie Ruo Mei) didn't speak a word of English (as detailed in chapter 1). As much as she was kind and great at her job, she did not seem too keen on children. She would not even tease a 'peek-a-boo' to our oldest daughter. After working for us for almost two years, the head of housekeeping informed me that Ruo Mei Ayi would be leaving and they would give us a new Ayi.

In came Hu Ayi who was clearly more familiar with children and loved their company. Being pregnant with our second baby at the time, this was the kind of person I needed. Like Ruo

Mei, she didn't speak English but by this time I had taken some Chinese language classes and could jumble my way through the day speaking Mandarin with her. She in fact challenged me to speak more Chinese because she was so sweet and talkative and engaged me in conversation every day. She was fantastic with both the baby and our oldest daughter, and although taking care of babies wasn't in her job description, she would often play with ours if I needed to take that all-too-important new-mum nap in the afternoon, or wanted to quickly go somewhere. She walked in every morning carrying something for us – oranges (*jú zi*), apples (*píng guo*), deep-fried dough sticks (*yóu tiáo*), bananas (*xiāng jiāo*), steamed buns (*bāo zi*) etcetera. She spent hours with our baby in the playground, entertaining and playing with her. Our daughter's first few words were all in Chinese and that is thanks to Hu Ayi.

She also prepared dumplings (*jiao zi*) and many other Chinese dishes that we enjoyed so much. My children were so fond of her and our baby's face lit up every morning she walked into the house. When we left China, we all cried in utter sadness. We miss her a lot.

Lebanon

WHEN THE AVERAGE LEBANESE sees a Black person, the first thing that comes to their mind is 'Maid'. Lebanon is home to over 250,000 migrant domestic workers (MDWs), according to Amnesty International. Most of them come from Africa, some come from South and South East Asian countries and the majority of them are women. There have been concerns for their well-being and how badly they are treated in some of the households they work, especially under the 'Kafala' system, which ties the legal residency of the worker to the contractual relationship with the employer. This means that even when these maids want to leave their employment, it is almost impossible because they technically cannot work anywhere else. Those that manage to leave the employment usually have their travel documents confiscated by the employer, leaving them illegal in the country and yet unable to return to their countries of origin. I have met a few maids in Beirut with shocking stories of not being paid a salary for years, being beaten by their 'boss' and in two instances, the girls were almost killed.

With this in mind, I initially felt uncomfortable having a housekeeper, not knowing what kind of measures my husband's office took to make sure they were employed legally and treated fairly. Turns out that the office vets the recruitment agencies and makes sure the maids get all befitting employment benefits, rights and security.

So, in came Safiya; a beautiful young girl from Ethiopia. Small problem though – she only spoke Arabic and Amharic (an Ethiopian dialect), with just one or two words in English. I was smacked in the face with a dizzying wave of Déjà vu. Not another language block. Not again! I had just gotten out of the Mandarin language 'conundrum' in Beijing. In Lebanon, I had expected to get someone who was able to speak English or, at the very least, French which is one of the three official languages in both Lebanon and our home residence Belgium. But alas, with Safiya I was back to pantomime gestures and mimicking.

This old head of mine had had enough of these non-Latin languages, thankyouverymuch. I was prepared to learn the very minimal, the basic 'Marhaba' and 'Keefak' type of Arabic but not narrating poems or using Arabic idioms. Mind you, I was very happy that our children were being exposed to these languages. It is a huge advantage and we encouraged them immensely, getting private tutors to help the oldest one become better with her Arabic and French. Safiya was so sweet and polite and with time, we understood each other through 'Google Translate', the few Arabic words I managed to learn and the few English words she spoke. We later changed to another housekeeper when we moved to another apartment. Senti was also from Ethiopia. She spoke better English and she was very kind.

Wherever we went in Lebanon, people assumed I was a maid and /or nanny to my kids because I am African. It was quite amusing to see people's faces when we walked into a restaurant and my husband was the one happily pushing the pram or feeding the baby. They probably wondered how he (my presumed boss) could let me get away with this. Hah!

Julie
Zimbabwe

WE MOVED INTO a lovely house in Harare that we called home for the three years we resided in the city. Located in a decent residential area called Ballantyne Park, it was cosy with perfectly manicured gardens. At the back of the house was a separate self-contained annex and in it were tenants who had lived on the premises for many years. These tenants were our 'inherited' employees.

To our surprise, the house also came with two dogs; a German Shepherd called Scotch and a huge Ridgeback called Whisky (no idea if the previous owners enjoyed a glass or too many of these 'beverages'). For those who might not know, Ridgebacks (also known as the African Lion Hound) are strong, muscular native breeds of South Africa specially bred by Boer farmers to hunt wild animals like lions. Scotch and Whisky were good and friendly – albeit scarily big – dogs that we were happy to keep around. However, our own dog Simba was soon joining us from Kampala and although Simba wouldn't hurt a fly, we figured there would be some dominance struggles between the three dogs, so we unfortunately had to re-home good ol' Whisky (the dog, not the drink).

Before long, our Simba arrived. He was a sweet, super friendly Golden Retriever but also the most 'useless' dog when it came to protecting us – and I say this with fondness. All he did was chew on our shoes or fall for anyone that gave him a cuddle and a rub. Imagine how easy it would be for robbers to gain entry to our home – a good old rub and Simba would hand them the keys and security codes to the house. Nevertheless, he was so adorable!

So back to our 'inherited' employees. This inheritance issue was imposed upon us but given the economic situation in Zimbabwe at the time, we were not about to deprive them of their jobs and livelihood and besides, they were in their home and we were the visitors. So, we rolled along with them, a decision we never regretted.

Juliet was a 5ft 10 no-nonsense giant of a lady in her mid 50's whose chores were mainly cooking and laundry. Tendai, Juliet's sister cleaned and tidied up while her husband was the gardener. They were kind, warm and very helpful.

South Africa

MOST EXPATS PREFERRED to employ migrant workers over South Africans in their homes. Word was that immigrants (from Malawi, Zambia, Zimbabwe or Mozambique) were more honest and trustworthy than the South African nationals (of course, we all know that honesty has nothing to do with one's nationality – but that was the word on the 'streets').

Our house helpers in Johannesburg were Zimbabweans but this was pure coincidence – we were not favouring Zimbabweans over other nationalities nor were we biased over trust and honesty issues with South Africans. It just so happened that there was an influx of Zimbabwean workers in South Africa at the time. Zimbabwe had seen its well-documented fair share of political and economic turmoil forcing many Zimbabweans to flee from their country in search of jobs in order to support themselves and their families back home. And where better to go than to Africa's economic giant – South Africa.

With many Zimbabweans employed in various job sectors

in South Africa, native South Africans took to the streets in protest and this led to the xenophobic attacks we saw in 2008 in many major cities like Durban, Johannesburg and Cape Town, with many losing their lives and property. Needless to say, it was disheartening to see these people – victims of political mismanagement back home – being knocked about yet again with these attacks. Many were highly skilled people with promising careers that they were forced to give up back home.

Prior to leaving her home town of Harare, our housekeeper/nanny was a certified nurse employed in one of the big hospitals in Harare. Our part-time gardener was a qualified medical doctor who circumstantially, tended to weeds and mowed lawns instead of caring for patients. These were just a couple of examples; there were so many other Zimbabweans whose hopes and dreams were ruined by a failing government, leaving them no choice but to flee their home country and find other means to feed and support their families.

Madagascar

WHEN WE HIRED JOCELYN, her basic tasks were cleaning and nanny duties. Ambitious and a fast learner, she had the desire to cook a variety of exotic dishes. I taught her a few recipes (I am an average cook but I have got some recipes up my sleeve) and, together with a few cook books in my kitchen drawer, she began making magic in the kitchen. *Qu' est-ce que c'était bon!*

Now, I embrace the fact that I am not the best cook around (don't judge). But neither am I a horrible one. While some men and women can casually and easily discuss *Boeuf Bourguignon,* or a *Pain Perdu aux Zestes D'orange*, I need a couple of days to find a small burst of inspiration to make one simple *Coq au vin.*

She was also highly knowledgeable on plant-based medicines. Sometimes she 'doctored' our kids when they had minor ailments like a cold or tummy ache, boiling up a few plant and flower concoctions and administering them to the kids. These concoctions worked most of the time. With her ambitious spirit and eagerness to learn more, she landed an assistant chef position at a restaurant after our departure. I couldn't be prouder of her.

Guinea

IT HAD ALWAYS BEEN a breeze finding domestic help while on missions abroad. But then we met Aline in Conakry and the good luck spell was broken. In the end, it came down to fourth-time-lucky charm before we found 'the one'.

Housekeeper Number 1

We always move with our household items wherever we go on missions. Needless to say, the packing and unpacking is always a hassle that takes a few weeks or up to a month before everything is unpacked and is in the right place. In Conakry, we received our shipping container with our personal effects and I was in dire need of a hand with the unpacking. Anybody who has moved homes will know how stressful this can be.

I had called Aline earlier and asked her to come over and help me with this task. She arrived at the planned time, waltzing in with a 36-inch Brazilian weave on her head (weaves and wigs are a big deal in this part of the world) and her casual jeans and T-shirt. That 'lifting and unpacking boxes' memo had clearly been lost somewhere because while we pushed and pulled boxes, furniture and other items, she found her pretty jeans-clad bottom a nice sweet sitting spot on our (newly unpacked) dining table and with zero self-reproach, began making casual conversation with the movers who were busy lifting items into the apartment. She watched us sweat while she comfortably swung her dangling legs on the table. The cheek!!! Needless to say, we asked her to leave and told her we would contact her. Your guess if we actually did!

Housekeeper Number 2

She came highly recommended by my husband's colleague. So, full of anticipation, hubby gave her a call and asked her for a meeting at our apartment. A tap on the door a few hours later and I enthusiastically opened it. Standing at the doorway was a beautiful lady wearing a long, elegant, figure-hugging-in-all-the-right-places colourful wax-printed dress. She wore subtle make-up and on her head a long (Brazilian, I am guessing) weave. I politely offered my *bonjour* to which she responded with a curious stare and began 'sizing' me up, giving me a look-over, from head to bottom. For a moment, I didn't understand why she would react like this to a stranger, and I was kind of offended. But then it hit me that with the state of unpacking we were in, coupled with my oversized, worn-out but comfortable dress, she must have thought I was just another help in the house – and therefore direct competition for her. That, or she just didn't expect 'Monsieur' who had called her, to have a 'chic' in the house.

After our salutations at the door, she swiftly sashayed past me, heading straight to the living room.

"J'ai rendez-vous avec le patron" (I have a meeting with the boss), she announced.

I diligently informed her that I would go find *le patron.* 'Boss' arrived, greeted her and introduced me as his wife. For a second, she looked dumbfounded and confused. Out of courtesy, we carried on with the interview, asking her some general questions about her experience, salary and working hours among other things. The interview ended, I shook her hand and told her to have a nice day. She must have read in between the lines. A lesson to never judge a book by its (ragged dress) cover.

Housekeeper Number 3

I was quite fond of number 3. She was tidy and polite and I allowed myself to think, *finally. A good one.* But boy was I wrong! She was great to begin with. After working for just a few weeks however, we started noticing that some things in the house were going missing – money in particular. Our lovely chef Abdul who we loved and trusted, was never a suspect. But it was also hard to believe that this new girl could be a thief. Long story short, I played Inspector 'Clouseau' (without the comedy) and before long, she was caught in the act. Another one bites the dust!

Housekeeper Number 4

Kadhija was our sweet fourth-time-lucky charm. She did lack a few qualities – let's just say, a turtle was 'Usain Bolt' compared to her. But she was a warm soul, honest and kind and we couldn't ask for more, especially given our previous experiences.

They certainly give very strange names to diseases.

— PLATO

4
THE DOC WILL SEE YOU NOW
MEDICAL STORIES WHILE LIVING ABROAD

When we feel unwell, we often long for the comforts of the familiar; cosying up at home in a large woollen sweater and socks, nourishing our bodies with fluids and soups, having close family and friends around and having the family doctor or a hospital on speed dial, just in case things go to rack and ruin.

Living abroad is all fun and games until you or your loved ones inevitably get unwell and these 'home' comforts are out of reach.

It takes time, especially for the young ones to adjust to the food, water, and air in a new environment. In many developing countries, water for example, is not treated the same way as it is in developed countries. So, in comes all manners of bacteria, parasites and other bugs.

While our stories aren't exactly the 'tourist-deep-in-the-jungle-sick-with-Malaria' type of dramatic tales, we have had some medical and non-medical incidents one would not typically encounter in a Western setting.

Finding a hospital, especially one with a decent supply of

medication can be a challenge at times. So, we have become mobile pharmacies – packing all tribes of medications like allergy tablets, inhalers, antibiotics, antiseptic creams, insect repellents and over-the-counter pain relievers. We are also required to get a number of jabs before we relocate; rabies, Japanese encephalitis, Hepatitis A and B, Yellow fever, Tuberculosis and so on. Our International Certificate of Vaccination or Prophylaxis (ICVP) booklets are cluttered with stamps and vaccine stickers.

Julie
Guinea

LIVING IN A COUNTRY where an emergency call (medical or other) is received with instant emergency response is a privilege often taken for granted. That one phone call to the emergency services can have a whole team of police, paramedics and firefighters arrive on the scene within minutes – almost like in the movies. Unfortunately, this privilege is non-existent in certain countries where the conditions, infrastructure and professionalism of emergency services will render you speechless.

When it came to ZERO EMERGENCY RESPONSE Guinea was a 'winner'. You could only hope and pray to never encounter an emergency situation, especially one related to fire. A family we knew in Conakry once experienced a (fortunately) minor fire incident in their home that was caused by an electric short circuit. Naturally, they telephoned *les sapeurs-pompiers* (firefighters). The response from the fire department was; *Désolé, il n y a pas de carburant dans les camions. Si vous voulez qu'on vienne, il faut nous acheter du gazole,* meaning *Sorry, we don't have fuel for the fire trucks. We can only come over if you pay for the gas.* Lord! Luckily for the family, they managed to put out the fire themselves before it caused further damage.

One afternoon I picked my son from school and took him to (supposedly the 'best in town') dentist for a tooth cavity filling. She was of European descent. Her clinic seemed decent enough and from what I could see, had all the necessary equipment to do the job. My son sat down in the dental chair and she started examining him. After a brief moment, I realised that she was perspiring profusely with sweat droplets trickling down her face and onto my son's T-shirt. Unbothered and without a word, she continued to carry out the procedure. In the end, I was glad she did what was required and off we went. I later heard that the same dentist had mistakenly taken out the wrong tooth (a healthy tooth) of a patient who required an extraction. The rumour on the streets was that she often 'drunk' on the job. Needless to say, I looked for other dentists and luckily, there were a few other good options.

One day the daughter of a friend badly sprained her toe while doing sports at school. She was taken to the hospital and consulted with a doctor who immediately suggested a toe amputation. Devastated, my friend arranged to have her daughter's procedure done abroad. While in Europe, she was informed that the amputation was absolutely not necessary. Thankfully her pinkie toe is still intact.

Madagascar

THANKFULLY, we never had any major medical or unpredicted mishaps in Madagascar. Many Malagasy people rely predominantly on traditional /alternative medicine so most of our treatments were basically 'home-made'; courtesy of our lovely housekeeper. She was quite well-versed with various medicinal plants and she never hesitated to come up with concoctions for mild symptoms like colds and flu.

OUR HOUSEKEEPER IN COMOROS, Eméline was Malagasy as well. She was an elderly petite lady in her fifties with a physique and energy of a 20-year-old (there is definitely something good in those medicinal herbs and plants in Madagascar). She was also motherly and kind. Once, I hurt my lower back and it left me immobilised. She promptly ran to the nearest carpenter's workshop and got back with shredded wood shavings that she placed in boiling water for a few minutes. She then wrapped them in a thick towel and lay it on my lower back and gently massaged it. It was an instant relief and a couple of days later, the pain was gone.

When she heard any one of us sniff, cough or whiz, she was instantly there with a cup of honey, lemon, ginger and egg yolk (yuck) mixture.

One time, my husband caught a bad cold that came with a high fever and chills. Eméline brought to boil a pan filled with mango, lemon, eucalyptus and palm leaves, added chunks of limes and let him inhale the vapour for 10 minutes. Thereafter, he was to take a bath with the water from the boiled herbs and massage his body with the plants. While our bathroom smelled really good from all the herbs and plants, it could easily have been mistaken for a voodoo chief's hut, haha.

For three consecutive days, she came by with yet more heaps of plants and leaves that she had picked up on her way. By day 4, hubby was up and about with all his strength fully back. Although he was taking other medications (painkillers and antibiotics), I am convinced that 'Doctor' Eméline's treatment contributed greatly to his full recovery.

SOUTH AFRICA HAS, without a doubt, one of the best, most sophisticated and dependable health care systems in Africa. It was here that I first experienced the most painless dentist procedure ever – one that didn't even require any high-tech medical equipment. In past visits to dentists, I would be asked if I was allergic to anything, to which I would jokingly respond, "yes, to dentists". That initial injection that's applied to the gum is as painful as it is annoying. On this encounter in South Africa, I visited the dentist to have two of my molars removed because of the discomfort they caused me. The dentist was a kind and gentle lady of Indian descent. We discussed my concerns and how I 'dislike' dentists and she assured me that everything would go well. I lay on the inclined chair and she rubbed a jelly-like cream on my gum to numb the area. Three minutes later she injected the anaesthetic and I did not feel a thing, not even a slight prick! She probably reserved that jelly-like cream for toddlers and children but it didn't matter that I was a grown adult woman, it worked like magic.

One day, out of the blue, I developed an acne breakout. Since I was way past the puberty stage (early 30's to be exact) I figured it was a medical issue and I consulted a dermatologist who prescribed Corticosteroids, other drugs and topical creams. My patience was running out when a month and a half later I was not seeing any improvement. Frustrated and desperate, my quest for a clearer skin led me to plan B. I turned to an esthetician for advice who proposed regular microdermabrasion treatments using natural plant-based products. Amazingly, after a mere two weeks, I noticed gradual improvement and within two months, my skin was spotless. According to her, I have sensitive skin, she advised me to steer away from industrial skincare products that are usually packed with harsh chemicals. I have henceforth favoured natural skincare products – an experience that led me to study an organic skincare course and create a handmade skincare line using natural ingredients.

My Miscarriage Journey

A year after our move to Zimbabwe (our first expat relocation together), my partner and I decided it was a good time for us to try for a baby so I threw out all the contraceptives and let nature take its course. A couple of months later, I started to experience prolonged periods that prompted me to consult a gynaecologist. A medical test revealed that I was going through an early pregnancy loss. I had gotten knocked up and had not even realised it! This was the first miscarriage and it happened so quickly, I had no time to let the idea of being pregnant, the baby nursery and all the joyous ideas and daydreaming sink in.

The second time I got pregnant was when we moved to South Africa. With my period over two weeks late, I curiously took a home pregnancy test and voila! Two apparent lines appeared on the stick. We were ecstatic. Eight weeks into the pregnancy, I began to spot lightly but didn't think much of it until the spotting gradually progressed. I scheduled a rendezvous with my gynaecologist and after an examination, she confirmed that it was a non-viable pregnancy.

Not again , I cried! My hopes had been high this time round and I had started imagining gooey baby things in my head.

It is not your fault she assured me, trying to comfort me. Her words fell on deaf ears. I was crashed. I walked out of her chambers with a prescription for pills meant to pass the embryo naturally. During the process, that lasted days, I had to come to terms with the fact that I was carrying (rather miscarrying) a child I was never going to meet.

On realising we were pregnant once again, I went for an ultrasound and all was well. *Third time lucky!* I thought. I experienced the common pregnancy symptoms: nausea, weakness and general lethargy that made me want to stay in bed all day. With enthusiasm, I shared the good news with my closest people and looked forward to the 12 weeks ultrasound check. My gynae was a lovely Kenyan lady who liked to engage her patients in small talk. The appointment for the 12-week ultrasound check arrived and she was being her chatty-self with us as she moved the scan wand around my belly. When she suddenly stopped chatting, I immediately sensed something was wrong. Her eyes were fixed on the ultrasound screen and her demeanour had changed. She looked up at me and revealed the painful news, she could not detect any foetal heartbeat. In that second, I felt like my own heart beat was gone too. I cried with so much anguish. My heart broke.

After I composed myself, she proposed the option of letting my body miscarry naturally or go for a D&C (a dilation and curettage; an operation to remove the foetus). I told her I needed a few days to decide – I suppose I was still in denial that this was happening yet again, and still had a tiny glimmer of hope that the ultrasound might have been faulty and that the baby was OK. After a few torturous days of walking around with a lifeless foetus and unbearable grief, I accepted what was. Psychologically and emotionally, I needed this ordeal to be over with and move on. I scheduled a D&C. As I lay on the hospital bed waiting for the general anaesthesia to be administered, I was in a deep pit of grief. I woke up in the recovery room after the surgery and bawled my eyes out. Looking straight up to the ceiling, I drew some comfort from my partner's hand. In silence, we just held hands; there was no need for words. All our hopes and plans were out of the window.

A few months after the D&C, we were pregnant AGAIN. You can only imagine the nerves, fear and apprehension we felt. I did not dare reveal the news to any family member or friend; not even to my mum and best friend. We waited until after the 18-week mark before we could reveal the news to very few people. After the previous recurring miscarriages, I was anxious throughout this pregnancy. I woke up every day hoping and praying my baby's heart was beating strongly. I was holding on to my faith – and my breath. To occupy me and keep my thoughts positive, I kept a diary of the pregnancy. Every time I jotted something in the diary, I was being reminded of how far we had come and how close we were to holding our longed-for baby.

Here are a few excerpts from my detailed pregnancy diary:

> **Sunday, 15 March 2009**: I was very inspired in church today. The theme was Faith. *Faith will always sustain you. When you pray for something, shut out all the distractions and negative information and let your faith soar.* How comforting.
>
> **Wednesday, 18 March**: You kicked several times this morning. It always makes me smile. Went for Aqua aerobics and really enjoyed it.
>
> **Friday, 20 March:** Pilates class at the gym. I called my girlfriends and told them I was pregnant. One of them says she had actually dreamt I was pregnant, how coincidental (*do you remember that day, Pearl?* ;-)
>
> **Tuesday, 24 March:** 19 weeks.

Wednesday, 25 March: Went to volunteer at the Children's home. We fed and bathed the babies. Little Terence was not there this time. He found adoptive parents. I am so happy for him. What a fulfilling experience. Had time to go to the gym later in the day.

Tuesday, 31 March: 20 weeks!!!! Halfway there, Thank you God.

Thursday, 2 April: Appointment at the gynae and found out we are blessed with a BOY! All is well. You are a big healthy boy. We are thinking of calling you Nathan after your grandfather.

Between 17 April and 11 July: Every part of my body is 'growing', even my nose is participating in the 'growth'.

Sunday, 12 July 2009: Your grandma arrived today from Uganda. I am happy she is here. I missed her very much.

Monday, 17 August 2009: 40 weeks: Our due date and MY birthday today. Celebrated at home with family. Papa prepared us a special delicious meal. I appreciate him so much, bless him.

Friday, 21 August 2009: YOU ARE HERE. We are on cloud nine. I can't stop staring at you. Where have you been all my life?

Very early that Friday morning in Morningside Clinic, Johannesburg, our baby was born. He arrived at 3.20AM, weighing 3.67 kilograms and 55 centimetres tall. Our son arrived via an unplanned Caesarean. I was ready to go the natural way (with epidural of course, *thank you very much!*) but nature took another turn. For three full hours, I stayed dilated at nine centimetres and the gynaecologist started to get concerned for the baby who was getting tired. She announced that my pelvis was too narrow for the baby to be born naturally and the only alternative was an emergency C-section. I was immediately whisked to the theatre where the nurses prepared me for surgery. It felt like minus 20 degrees in the operating room, I was trembling from the cold but my pleas for a cover went unheard. Shockingly there was no screen placed between us (hubby and I) and the gynae and her nurses. The surgery was a live show with hubby bravely watching every detail and me avoiding to look lest I fainted. I was awake throughout the procedure chatting with hubby and the only thing I felt was a weird sensation similar to food being churned or a dishwasher being operated inside my belly. Finally, we heard that CRY! He was everything I dreamed of, a bouncing baby boy with a rugged beautiful face. His toothless smile, coos and babbles warmed our hearts and helped me heal from the past grief.

I am forever grateful for the two healthy children I have been blessed with but sometimes, I can't help but wonder how the ones we previously lost would have looked like. Would they have looked more like me or their dad? There were times when I blamed myself and wondered if I had done something wrong to trigger the losses, although I now fully realise that it was never my fault. I learned that it is OK to mourn and deal with heartaches in the best way you can.

There is a staggering number of women (relatives, friends and friends of friends) who have experienced one or multiple miscarriages. A dear friend of mine opened up to me and expressed her personal struggles. She experienced seven miscarriages before deciding to take the adoption route. This encounter presented me with a whole new level of appreciation, empathy and respect for all the women who have done everything in their capacity to become mums. I honour those who have transitioned to motherhood and those who have given up all hope despite the setbacks. And to the medical professionals who comfort and help us in our despair.

Pearl
Bangladesh

WE HAD MANAGED to 'dodge' the Dengue Fever in the first year of living in Dhaka. However, with its prevalence in this part of the world and the sheer insane amount of Dengue-causing pesky little mozzies around, it was inevitably a matter of time before we got it, just like Malaria in Africa – and I should know. Growing up in Uganda, I spent a chunk of my school years constantly being 'med-evacuated' from boarding school because of Malaria.

One afternoon in Dhaka, my then four-year-old daughter said, "Mama, I'm not feeling well". An hour or so later and with all the telltale signs, I called the nearest hospital and made an appointment to rush her in for tests. On arrival at the hospital, we were quickly ushered in to meet with a paediatrician. At this point, my daughter was throwing up everywhere and her head was hurting so badly she could barely open her eyes. The doctor promptly sent us to the laboratory for tests after which they sent us home and told us to wait for the results – I have no idea why they just couldn't keep us there until the results came back.

We were just getting back into the apartment when the hospital called and confirmed the Dengue Fever diagnosis. They told us to immediately get back to the hospital for admission. Every bump in the road made her scream out in pain from the throbbing headache she had that seemed to be getting worse by the minute. I was beside myself with worry and so was my husband. The journey back to the hospital took all but 10 minutes – miraculously there was not too much traffic – but it felt like an hour. On arrival, she was immediately admitted and put on an IV drip. Thankfully, within a day, she started to feel better. We stayed in the hospital for four days, being cared for by a wonderful team of nurses and a great doctor, until we were given the all-clear and discharged from the hospital.

United Hospital Dhaka is a big, clean medical centre with very professional and helpful staff (save for the cleaners who looked on as my daughter vomited all over the bathroom floor and they didn't bother cleaning it up immediately). The doctors we saw were very professional and checked on us frequently, assuring us we were in good hands.

China

"OH, YOUR DAUGHTER is so cute." Thanks.

"Do you have other children?" No.

"Oh, why not?" I ... I ... I don't know.

"Are you planning on giving her a brother or sister?" Ahhhhh, none of your GD business?!

It is incessant isn't it? Questions from people, strangers even, asking when you are going to have kids or – if you already have one – when the next one is coming along. If you have two of the same sex, they'll be hammering on about how you need one child of the opposite sex 'to balance things out'. Little do they know about your struggles.

Anyone who has attempted to get pregnant will attest to the sheer madness and pain the waiting can sometimes cause. It can turn one into a 'more-cuckoo-than-a-clock-factory' crazy person. Calculating your fertile days or taking your basal temperature becomes a routine. Peeing on a stick, waiting for a smiley face that is subtly screaming at you to *do the deed within 72 hours or the egg goes away,* making sure that your bodily fluids are saying 'ripe', putting your other half on so much pressure to 'perform' and finally peeing on another stick two weeks later – this time waiting for two magical lines to appear and confirm you are with child. Having to repeat this over and over again can be tiring and often depressing – just like being told to *wait ... it will happen when you least expect it.* You really lose your s**t.

Our first pregnancy was text-book perfect; I fell pregnant the month we started trying, had a wonderful, stress-free pregnancy and a seamless natural delivery. I was ready to push out 10 more kids. When we moved to Dhaka, Bangladesh, our oldest daughter had just turned 2.5 years. We had discussed giving her a sibling as soon as we settled into our new home and obviously assumed it would be a cinch, just like with the first pregnancy and birth.

Surely those ovaries are still healthy and warm and so is the sperm, I mused silently.

But, nature – and God – had a biiiig belly laugh at our plans.

We started 'trying'. And month after month after month, we saw only one line on that pee-stick, even after some telltale signs (*gosh, these boobs are huge and they sure do hurt more this month*) and other misread signs (*did I just feel nauseated? Do I want to throw up? Am I ...?*). I kept whispering to myself, *this is my month.* But when those months turned into one year and a few months, I cried in desperation, seeing my plans go out of the window. So, I made the decision to talk to a fertility specialist and see if something was wrong.

Notice the *"I"* pronoun, because my husband thought I was going a bit coo-coo and over thinking the whole thing and was just worrying for nothing. He told me that this was a clear sign that there's something not right at the time, and that we should just let nature take its course; *if it happens it happens and if not, it is OK.* Of course my coo-coo head didn't listen to him. I visited Apollo hospital, a renowned medical centre in Dhaka, with the fertility expert there considered one of the best around. I made the first visit to the fertility clinic by myself because I wanted to talk to the doctor and get any necessary tests done and if required, I would make an appointment for my husband to get checked out too.

On the day of the appointment, I was at the hospital main entrance by 7am – and so were over 5,000 people with their eyes all trained on me as soon as I walked in (did I mention people in Bangladesh love to stare and aren't afraid to do so openly?).

Inside the reception area, hundreds of people were queuing up at the cashier desks and lab collection points – it was busy. In this sea of people, I couldn't find the directions to the fertility clinic until a kind man saw my state of confusion and offered to direct me accordingly.

Located on the first left turn from the reception area, it was a small space – certainly small for the number of patients there that day. There was nowhere to sit with every available seat occupied and many people standing. Some were impatiently shoving their folders in the doctor's assistant's face, all desperately hoping their name would be read out next if their folder was on top of the pile. Who needs appointments right? I didn't have a folder to add to the pile but luckily, the doctor's assistant called out my name a few minutes after I arrived. She invited me into a side room to take my vitals and asked me a few questions.

Less than an hour later, I was ushered into the doctor's office. He was a very pleasant man who made me feel immediately at ease. Every wall inch on the right side of his desk was covered with pictures of 'success stories'; smiling, content parents with their long-awaited bundles of joy – twins, triplets, boys, girls – all thanks to science and in part to this man. It was heartwarming. We got chatting about why I was there; "just a check-up to see that everything is ok with me", I told him. I made it clear from the beginning that under no circumstances were my husband and I looking at doing In Vitro Fertilisation (IVF), no matter what the reason for this sudden 'infertility' turned out to be. He ordered some blood work to be done and told me to come back two days later when the results were in.

Just like most large medical centres in Dhaka, Apollo Hospital was an extremely modern and efficient hospital that had almost all medical departments. This was another plus for our stay in Dhaka. We were never worried about finding a hospital. The only downside to medical services in Dhaka was the ambulance service. They did run a decent ambulance assistance but they so often got stuck in the infamous Dhaka traffic that it was almost pointless to use them. Every Time I saw an ambulance in traffic, I said a prayer for whoever was being transported – not only to get better but to make it to the hospital in the first place.

After four years of trying, a 'missed' miscarriage and two failed rounds of IntraUterine Insemination (IUI), we completely gave up on trying for a second baby. There was certainly a feeling of disappointment and some very hard, ugly days but we knew we had tried. Besides, we were already blessed beyond words with our oldest daughter. A few years later, I did fall pregnant naturally and gave birth to our second baby girl, as detailed below.

ONE MORNING, two years after moving to Beijing, I was feeling a bit off. A cold? Flu? Or had I over-indulged in all those cocktails we had had on our trip to Hong Kong two weeks earlier during the Chinese New Year and my birthday celebrations? Or was it the wine that I'd had a week later for Alyssa's birthday dinner and a night out with Vero and Ruby?

But ... hold on ... my period is late, I thought. But there's no way ... I mean ...

I bought several tests and put them away for one day, to see if it was another false alarm. When the painters failed to show up the next day, I bolted the bathroom door shut and peed on a stick. Gosh, it was a while since I had peed on one. Three seconds later. A big fat POSITIVE. Oh, stars and garters!!! 'Unexpected' doesn't begin to describe it. We had tried to have a second baby for years with no luck and we had given up. What a beautiful surprise this was. For us for sure but especially for our oldest daughter who had longed for a sibling for years. Naturally, at this time, it was too early to get all excited because we had had our hopes dashed before.

With this pregnancy news, I knew exactly which hospital I would go to in Beijing, and so I made the first appointment. Beijing United Hospital is a world-class facility with several branches scattered around Beijing city. So, I was sure I was in good – albeit expensive – hands (thank God for medical insurance).

The first hospital visit was for a blood test after which the pregnancy was confirmed. Almost eight weeks along. Several cries and ecstatic air punches, later, it started sinking in that we were going to be parents again. We were invited to go back at nine weeks gestation for the first scan. On this visit, we saw an obstetrician/gynaecologist (OB/GYN) who spoke good

English and was very professional. In casual conversation, she asked us what sex we would prefer to which, without hesitation, my husband replied, *"a girl"*. The doctor seemed quite startled because she knew our oldest was a girl and probably expected us to say, *"a boy"*.

In China and many other cultures in the world, there is a well-documented preference for boys – something I don't understand. Anyway, at the end of the day it really didn't matter because, cliché or not, a healthy baby is what any parent wants, right?

Facilities in many of Beijing's hospitals are better than most in the world, so there was never a doubt that I would be in good hands throughout the pregnancy in China. So, we made all the necessary arrangements for the birth later that year. Unfortunately, there were quite a few challenges that in the end convinced us to travel back to and give birth in Belgium.

The first challenge came when I booked for my three-month scan – that which gives most parents the all-clear to shout the pregnancy news from the rooftops, if you so wish. This was the scan where we were finally going to tell our oldest daughter that she was going to be a big sister. We were waiting for this scan with so much anticipation. A day before the planned scan, I got a call from the hospital, with a polite nurse on the other end informing me that the scan would have to be cancelled.

"Why?" I asked.

She informed me that according to the calculations, I would *only* be 11 weeks and six days pregnant – just one day short of 12 weeks. I thought it was a joke. One day short of 12 weeks and they wouldn't give me a scan. As if the machine would not operate unless I was exactly 12 weeks along. This reminded me of that 'Little Britain' TV sketch with David

Walliams's character, Carol Beer always saying "Computer says No" for every request someone makes. Yep, things in China can be pretty strict. If the scan HAS to say 12 weeks, it HAS to be done at 12 weeks, not a day earlier (I suspect not even hours earlier) otherwise *computer says no.*

The second challenge was how difficult it can be to find out the gender of your baby. In China, all pregnant women above the age of 35 have to do the Non-Invasive Prenatal Test (NIPT) that checks for foetal abnormalities. This is recommended to be done before the all-important 12-week scan. In fact, many Chinese are required to do the more evasive one of taking fluid directly from the amniotic sac. Being over 35 at the time, I 'qualified' for the test, but I chose the noninvasive blood test. The NIPT reveals the gender of the baby and in Europe, they are able to tell you, if you so wish. In China, it is strictly forbidden for doctors to tell expectant parents the gender of their baby due to previous gender selection abortions. We always want to know the baby's gender as soon as possible – we are very impatient, you see. The fact that we would not be able to find out the sex also played a small role in our decision to give birth in Europe.

The other challenge was the language and communication barrier. Many hospitals that cater to the expatriate community in Beijing have staff that speak good English. However, it is still not perfect and one time I had to use a nurse as a translator because the doctor on duty that day did not speak good English. So, while I was fully confident in the care they would give me in Beijing, I was a tad worried that communication would be a bit of a problem.

In any case, we had already booked our annual summer holidays back to Belgium that year, so we decided that me and our oldest daughter would stay on in Belgium until the baby arrived. We welcomed our second daughter in November that year.

Chinese hospital facilities are world class. I didn't go to any local Chinese hospital but I was told that they are even better than the private hospitals. Many foreigners go to private hospitals because of the language barrier they would otherwise encounter in public hospitals.

Lebanon

COVID, COVID, COVID.

If 'depressing' and 'frustrating' were people, their faces would look exactly like COVID-19.

When we arrived in Beirut in 2021, COVID-19 still had its nasty face plastered all over the world, with the latest and highly infectious variant at the time – OMICRON – doing the rounds. Schools and businesses were open in Lebanon but all preventative measures remained largely in place.

As soon as our youngest daughter started daycare, she got her first dose of 'toddler germs'. Almost every week, she came home with either a fever or with some seriously stuffy, runny nose before she would inevitably pass that on to us. It was unrelenting. Four months in, after yet another bout of stuffy noses, fever and coughs, we all thought we had caught the usual flu bugs from her yet again. When we noticed the symptoms were slightly different from the usual, we tested for COVID-19 and the result came back positive.

"Here goes quarantine number 20 for us", we sighed with annoyance. We remained quarantined in our apartment for over 15 days. We went for tests on day 10 and 12 and our results were still showing positive. Finally, on day 14 we got a negative.

COVID-19 test centres in Beirut are many, all well-managed and easily accessible.

Best thing in this otherwise annoying time was the fact that we lost our sense of smell due to COVID-19 and that meant we couldn't smell our toddler's 'kaka bomb diapers'. Every parent will understand the bliss in this. ;-)

Lebanon's power supply was under so much strain due to the economic crisis in the country at the time. Hours-long power cuts affected many businesses, including major hospitals that were on the verge of running out of diesel fuel used for their back-up generators. Lives were on the line. Before the economic crisis, Lebanon had world-class doctors and health facilities and was a regional leader in standard private and public healthcare, cosmetic and plastic surgery. By 2021, many of these healthcare professionals had left the country in search of better pay cheques.

In general, the formidable Lebanese Red Cross was still operational, with highly reputed and fast emergency response and assistance. Many pharmacies around Beirut also had a very decent stock of over-the-counter medication as well as a huge assortment of personal hygiene care products, both imported and locally produced.

There seems to be a specialist clinic or hospital on every corner in Beirut. Everywhere you look is a Doctor's practice with an ophthalmologist, cardiologist, dentist, orthodontist, stomatologist, dermatologist, gynaecologist or paediatrician. Now, whether these specialists were actually inside the clinics is another matter because as I mentioned earlier, many had escaped the economic crisis for greener pastures outside Lebanon. It was however comforting to know that they existed and many of them reputedly so.

You have brains in your head, you have feet in your shoes, you can steer yourself any direction you choose.

— DR. SEUSS

5
SCHOOL TALES
MEET THE PARENTS, TEACHERS AND CHILDREN

On any first day of school, parents and children are usually riding on emotional waves of anxiety and excitement. On a first day of school in a brand-new country, these emotional waves run amok with the confusion of simultaneously having to adjust to a new place, a new school and new people.

Most children are not fussy, they form friendships faster than adults. We tend to be a little picky and are bent towards meeting people with whom we share mutual interests and have a positive connection with. Even for a fairly sociable person, first encounters can feel quite awkward and it can take a while to find your 'people' but once you do, it is enriching.

Via school parents, our spouses' workplace, other expat spouses, neighbours or friends of friends, this relocation road has woven some great long-lasting friendships for us.

While living abroad, our children often attend international schools. This is not because we have bag-loads of money – our bank balance certainly proves we don't. In international school settings, we all come from different backgrounds, different countries, speak different languages and our one binding factor is a unique understanding of the transient culture we are adapting to.

The international school community and environment can be a great escape from the perplexing uncertainties of a new country and can help you feel less 'out of place'.

PEARL
Bangladesh

OUR OLDEST DAUGHTER was three years old when she started her first year in Pre-Kindergarten 3 at the American International School of Dhaka (AISD). I was a mixed bag of emotions seeing my baby girl go off to a real school for the first time, worried about how she would adjust to a new country, a new school and new friends.

A few weeks before school started, we visited it for a day of orientation and we met the homeroom teachers and teaching assistants as well as a few other parents. So, we knew our way around the school before classes started.

As I dropped her off to her class that first school morning, there was the expected shyness and hesitation but soon she was off, joining her new classmates and forgetting I was even there. It was then my turn to meet fellow parents.

I walked from the Pre-K section of the school, through the big rotunda, past the reception area before finding my way to the elementary school cafeteria. The cafe was teeming with excited chatter amongst parents, most of whom were seemingly well acquainted with one another. It made me feel even more uncertain and out of place. I realised quickly that I had to break into this mound sooner rather than later. I needed to SURVIVE. PRONTO!!! It didn't take long before I got chatting to a few people, some of whom were also new to Dhaka.

The school itself was a calm oasis in the busy Dhaka life. With several playgrounds, gymnasiums, libraries and a swimming pool, it was a wonderful facility, with engaging and friendly staff. Many of the school facilities were accessible to all parents so it became yet another meet-up place for a catch-up, whiling away the hours while waiting for the kids to finish their after-school activities.

The school had bus drop-off and pick-up services which we made use of during the first year of school. However, sometime during the second year, the security situation in Dhaka became so precarious when extremists threatened to target American and other foreign entities and personnel in the capital. Our daughter's school was as American as they come – it was directly linked to the American Embassy in Dhaka and used diplomatic number plates on the school buses. This inevitably made it an apparently high target for extremists.

As word sipped through that the school could be a target, it understandably put everyone on edge. At first, the school and the embassy reassured us that they would employ the best security to ensure the utmost safety of the children and staff. This reassurance was in the form of hiring heavily armed security personnel to escort the buses to and from school every day; two armed security men on motorcycles in the front of each bus and two behind it. For added measure, they put another security agent inside each bus.

While this was done with the best intentions, it did nothing to reassure me or many other parents. Buses were still taking the same route, still getting stuck in the infamous Dhaka traffic. So, with all this added security, our children were sticking out like sore thumbs and were sitting ducks for these extremist goons.

A day or two after these measures were put in place, we resorted to taking our daughter to and picking her up from school with our driver – something she resented. You see, with the armed school bus escorts, she and her friends thought they were some sort of VIPs cruising around Dhaka with armed guards and all. She also missed being on the bus with her friends. In general though, the school security was extremely good and once inside the campus, we were never worried about the kids' safety.

We had been living in Bangladesh for two years when one summer day, a restaurant in the diplomatic area of Dhaka was attacked by over six machine gun and machete wielding extremists. Many people, mostly foreigners, were taken hostage for more than 24 hours and eventually all but four were brutally murdered (as described in Chapter 2).

We were in Belgium at the time for the summer holidays and we were subsequently forbidden from returning to Dhaka. And that's when our daughter joined the Belgium schooling system for the first time.

Duffel, Belgium (2016–2017)

DUFFEL IS A MEDIUM-SIZED, cosy, family-friendly precinct in the Dutch-speaking northern part of Belgium. It lies on the Nete River, about 20 minutes from the city of Antwerp and is home to around 17,000 people, including us. We have lived in Duffel for many years and our oldest daughter was born in the town. She attended a baby playgroup, a.k.a *Creche* a.k.a *kinderopvang* in Duffel from when she was around eight months old until we left for Dhaka, Bangladesh when she was 2.5 years old.

When we unexpectedly had to settle back in Belgium, my biggest worry was how this change would affect our daughter. She, like a lot of kids, is resilient but this was a huge change for all of us, let alone a five-year old. She had left Belgium after 2.5 years, had joined a new, English-speaking school – having previously spoken almost exclusively Flemish – and she had had to make new friends in Dhaka. Yet here we were, back to what for her was a new environment, even if she had been here before and it was our home. Furthermore, she didn't understand why we couldn't return to Dhaka, she hadn't said bye to her friends there, she barely remembered the baby friends she had met in playgroup in Duffel and while she spoke – and still speaks – fluent Dutch, English was now her dominant language yet Flemish was the language of instruction in Belgium.

I asked her one evening how she felt about it all. She shrugged and said that while she missed Dhaka, she was excited that we could easily travel to the United Kingdom to visit all her cousins with whom she is very close. One huge positive at least.

There was not much time to linger on the sadness of this terrible terrorist act or our confused thoughts and feelings. We had to quickly find a school for her. It was the middle of the summer holidays in Belgium and schools were not exactly open for business. Luckily, the principal for one of the schools near our home kindly made time for us, enrolled our daughter into the school system for the first time and gave us all the information we needed. It turned out that three of her former 'playmates' in Creche were also in the same school, including one whose mother, Stefanie, is a dear friend of mine. Another positive.

While the new school year in Dhaka started in early August, schools in Belgium usually open in the first week of September. So, we had quite a long summer and we were able to spend a month in the United Kingdom visiting my family.

Soon, it was the first day of school. The school entrance was abuzz with excited chatter. The children were all playing outside, happy to see their friends back after the long summer holidays. Parents were chatting to each other, many hurriedly, clearly rushing off to work. The homeroom teacher quickly came over to us and with an encouraging big smile, took our daughter by the hand and led her away to join other kids on the playground. Normally parents aren't supposed to stay around the school gate after the drop-off, but I couldn't help it. I lingered outside looking in, trying to see where she was. She had joined two girls on the playground and they seemed to be getting on quite well. Soon the bell rang and they all made lines behind their teachers before they were led inside their classrooms for the start of school.

I walked back to where I had parked my car, opened the door, sat inside and cried so hard, so hard that I started hyper-ventilating. Seeing my girl in a playground filled with kids she didn't know, yet all the kids seemed to know each other, was really hard for me. In most international schools abroad, it is slightly different because at the start of any given school year, you are sure that you won't be the only new parent or new child in the school or class. Orientation days in international schools are flowing full of new families. Here in Duffel, we seemed to be the only new family – at least from what I saw. I wondered how she would cope. Would she manage to speak Dutch the whole day? Would she make friends? Would she miss me?

Pick-up time rolled by. I was waiting at the school gate 45 minutes before the school day ended – I was that nervous. Would she be smiling or sad or indifferent? Not the latter please. I wanted emotions. Happy or sad because I would know how to deal with those. When she finally emerged, she was jumping and seemingly happy. She told me that her day had gone fantastic.

"The only thing I don't like", she noted, "is that the school doesn't have a swimming pool. We have to go to the public pool to swim".

Hmmmm, I chuckled, explaining to her that not every school has its own swimming pool and that having one is not a mark of excellence for a school. Not sure her 5-year old mind grasped what I was saying though.

The rest of the year went extremely well. She often chatted with her friends from Dhaka who, like us, were back in their own countries and dealing with similar changes and challenges. She knew that we were not the only ones going through this, and that helped. She joined a Saturday gymnastics class in Duffel and her cousin Bo took her swimming most weekends, so this kept her pretty busy. Stefanie, the creche mummy-friend whose daughter was in the same class as ours helped me enormously. Through her, I joined the parents' Facebook group, weekend activity groups and she introduced me to one of her friends Joelika, another easy-going wonderful soul. They always informed me about the news in the school community in case I had missed something. I always relied on their faces to make me feel less 'lost'.

One of my biggest challenges of settling back in Belgium was having to speak Dutch more often. In Dhaka, we had the Dutch expat club and lots of Dutch-speaking people but English was still the most spoken language. Being back in Belgium meant readjusting to speaking more Dutch than English. This may seem banal to some, but over the years I have struggled to remember what language to speak and where.

First off, Dutch is not my mother tongue. I had to learn to speak it when I moved to Belgium. I took intensive 5-days, 6 hour-per-day classes at the University of Antwerpen and gradually became comfortable speaking it. During this period of learning Dutch, my husband was working away a lot and I was mostly alone with our daughter in Belgium. She was speaking more Dutch than any other language, so I had to make sure that I spoke a bit of English and Luganda (my Ugandan local dialect) to her. When I should have been practising speaking Dutch with her, I was instead teaching her to speak English.

The only time I did speak Dutch was with my husband's family or our friends, but it wasn't near enough.

Just when I was getting the 'ang of it, we moved to Dhaka. And there, the tables turned. Since I am the parent that spends almost all day with the kids, I found myself having to switch to speaking more Dutch to our daughter because at this point, all TV programmes, school and homework was in English and she was now almost 'forgetting' her Dutch.

Luckily, Belgians are famous polyglots so I wasn't exactly lost in translation when I was back in Duffel but I still struggled.

Another challenge I faced back in Duffel was making friends. Constant relocation often means that most expat wives or husbands are stay-at-home parents. This is not always by choice – it is because of how difficult it is to find a job in a foreign country and our visas are sometimes restrictive in this. Often, we are not even sure of how many years we are going to be staying in a country. So, as stay-at-home parents, our school drop-offs may result in impromptu breakfasts and coffee breaks with other stay-at-home parents. There is often no hurry to go somewhere so you bond easily with one another.

Many families in Belgium have both parents working full-time. So, as I mentioned earlier, school drop-offs were very rushed. This meant I was dropping our daughter off at school in the morning, bumping into parents who offered a polite but quick *dag* (hi/bye) before hurrying off. It was quite lonely compared to Dhaka. Luckily, I had our family friends Sarah and Dirk, my sister-in-law Elke, her two daughters Sophie and Bo and 'Oma' Yvette who all helped me a lot and kept us company. I also had my dear sisters Margaret, Anna, Lucy, Dovic and my brothers Francis and Titah right across the channel in England. We chatted away for hours on end and they visited me as I did them. My mum and my other two sisters Betty and Juliet also visited us in Belgium, which was great.

Finally, we blinked and, what do you know? A year is over. *Finished! Fini! Gedaan!*

That summer, in front of family and friends, we finally got married (yes, we had been 'living in sin' all these years. *No judgements* ;-)). Soon after the wedding, we packed up again, said bye and landed in Beijing China, ready for new school drop-offs.

China

WHAT IS THAT SAYING about America and size? Go big or go home, right? Well, our daughter's new school in China, The International School of Beijing (ISB) was American ... and then some. They did go hammer and tongs here. Huge outdoor sports field and another indoor for the bad pollution days when kids would be unable to participate in sports activities outside. Three (or maybe more – I stopped counting) gymnasiums, huge swimming pool, massive libraries and cafeterias for elementary, middle and high school, a spacious theatre, more than five tennis courts and best of all, the wonderful staff. I was so excited to move to China, the mighty South-East Asian giant. I had always wanted to visit the country so to hear that we would be living in Beijing for several years was beyond exhilarating.

In terms of what to expect from schools, we had three years of 'practice' in Dhaka and Belgium, so I felt confident that I would quickly navigate my way around this new school system and integrate with people without a lot of hitches. As per norm, we were invited to the school for a day of orientation a week before school officially started. We lived downtown near the Central Business District (CBD) area of Chaoyang district in Beijing. The school was located in another district called Shunyi. It was roughly a 30-minute drive (without traffic) from our house to the school. Once at the school, we were taken for a quick tour, met many new parents and got everything we needed for our daughter's first day of class; school identity card, homeroom number and the name of her teacher.

Our daughter started Grade 1 a week later. We picked her up from school later that day and she excitedly showed us around the massive school grounds, the different play areas as well as her class. We were in awe.

If I thought that meeting new parents in Beijing was going to be as easy as it had been in Dhaka, Bangladesh, I was wrong. Although the school's student population is mostly international, parents in ISB are overwhelmingly Chinese. While the Chinese parents were so kind, warm and welcoming, many of them spoke little to no English and we, the foreigners spoke little to no Chinese. Many a times, I came across Chinese parents who would politely smile at me and clearly want to say a few more words but alas; *ni hui shuo zhong wen ma?* (do you speak Chinese?), they would ask me, to which I would reply, *wo bu hui shuo zhong wen* (I don't speak Chinese). Of course I would deliver this one-liner in the flattest, most toneless way. Polite end of conversation. I found these 'lost in translation' moments frustrating because there was a genuine crack at establishing a friendly chat which was always hindered by language.

Another challenge we faced in Beijing was the distance between our downtown apartment and the school. We unfortunately don't choose where we live while abroad – we have absolutely no say in it. My husband's work determines that and unfortunately it rarely considers families and what is best for children. So, we had a six-year old travelling on a school bus for over two hours to and from school every day. It was heavy. Many of the expat parents lived near the school (they clearly work for more considerate employers). This made any meet-ups, both for myself and for our daughter, almost impossible. Our daughter got home from school just after 4:30pm every day, so any plans for after-school activities or playdates with her friends became impractical.

In the end of course, I did meet a few parents, including some from the downtown Girl Scouts group, some through our downtown Church and many through our daughter's school friends.

In ISB as well as many other international schools in Beijing, learning Chinese is compulsory for every student with all of them given one-hour Chinese lessons every day. Now while I understand that Chinese is the most widely spoken language in the world, I still didn't appreciate the fact no other 'world' language was offered as an alternative. Many of us are transient in a country, for a maximum of four years before we move on to another country. Where else is one going to be able to practice the Mandarin they have learned in school apart from in China – unless you have Chinese parents of course. I found it rather illogical that other languages like French, Spanish or German were not offered in elementary school.

The staff at ISB however went out of their way to make everyone feel welcome. It is a top school, a truly superb place for an education and we feel extremely blessed to have been a part of the ISB community in China.

BY THE TIME WE ARRIVED in Lebanon in October 2021, schools had already been open for a month. Being a new school (yet again) for our oldest daughter, the same questions tormented me; Would she fit in and be able to adjust easily? I need not have worried.

Located near the Corniche that runs along the Mediterranean Sea shores of Beirut, the American Community School, Beirut (ACS) was a 15-minutes (very steep) walk from our apartment. On the first day of her attendance, we met her Grade 5 class teacher who is something of a legend for being one of the longest serving faculty members, an incredible teacher, and an even better human being. She was warm and welcoming and so was the rest of the staff.

At the end of the first day of school, I was eagerly waiting for our daughter at the school gate. She came outside smiling and chatting to some of her new classmates who all seemed lovely. Less than a week later, she was inundated with birthday and playdate invites. She was settling in very well and that is all that mattered to me. Time for me to meet other parents.

I first met many of them at a birthday party a classmate of our oldest daughter was organising. We easily started a conversation and they warmly welcomed me to Lebanon and to the school, promptly adding me to all relevant parent WhatsApp groups. Many gave me their private phone numbers so I could call them in case I needed anything in Lebanon.

Later on, I was invited to the school's International Parents' group where I met many other parents through regular dinner meetings.

One of the first things on my to-do list in Beirut was to get our second daughter into daycare – COVID-19 permitting. Since birth, she had only attended a playgroup in Beijing but attendance was periodic due to COVID-19 precautions and restrictions. In the playgroup, I had to stay with her for the hour we attended. While it was fun, I still longed for some serious 'me time'. I needed to get that *baby shark do-do-do-do* song and all those nursery rhymes out of my head for just a few hours. I needed to get her into a daycare for longer than three hours.

It wasn't long before I got one that was ideally located just a stone's throw from our apartment. I immediately got her registered and I was so happy that I would be getting a few hours on my own while she played and interacted with kids her age. She immediately liked it there.

There was never much interaction between the parents in the daycare. We never seem to drop the kids off or pick them up at the same time and when we did, it was always so hurriedly. What mattered most to me was how quickly she adapted to and loved it.

Julie
Madagascar

MY JOURNEY with the school parents began in Madagascar when my son who was six joined one of the three French primary Schools in Antananarivo. The road to the school parking was narrow with a steep descent and the traffic to get there was horrendous. Fortunately, there was a bus system with several drop-off and pick-up spots close to our home that alleviated those tiresome back and forth commutes.

We got to meet our son's teachers as well as some old and new parents that first school day. The 'old' parents evidently had their already-established social circles. As they chatted and laughed with each other, we kept to our little corner, smiling sheepishly, trying to not come across as unapproachable. Most parents seemed happier than the children – probably relieved that the kids were finally back in school. After a few formalities, we found our son's class, said hello to his new teacher; a petite and pleasant lady, and off we went.

In the school's compound, I noticed that many of the Malagasy school mums were meticulously clad in elaborate clothing and accessories. Some ladies were clearly on their way to work but as I learned later on, Malagasy ladies don't really need a special occasion to dress up to the nines. I admired their effortless elegance and consistency.

The acquaintances I made with some school mums were wonderful. They were the friendliest, warmest, fun-loving bunch of ladies with a zest that exuded energy and enthusiasm. Outside of school, we shared regular ladies-lunches, social events and some were my Zumba and yoga buddies.

My daughter was three year when she started pre-kindergarten at this cute little private school in Tana. The school adopted a 'guardian' system with well trained staff assigned to each class. On the first school day, we were welcomed by our daughter's assigned guardian, a friendly and bubbly lady. Our daughter took to her immediately which was a surprise given that she was quite reserved with strangers. She was obviously not the first child we had seen off to school but watching her play in the school's playground left me with the all too familiar feelings of separation anxiety, sadness and utter pride.

Her school organised diverse after-school activities, spectacular end-of-year tournaments, sports events, carnivals etcetera. Parents were pleasantly entertained with theatrical performances and musicals twice a year, usually before the big summer and Christmas holidays. My favourite of these events was the Disco themed event. Watching my daughter performing 'Stayin' Alive', with her big curly afro hair and bell bottom pants warmed my heart.

In the school parking lot was a cosy cafeteria with the most sinful pastries and a fountain overflowing with creamy chocolate fondue. It was a common meeting place for parents, where we chatted, drank café lattes, and abused our calorie intake and our waistlines as we waited to pick up the kids. Oh, good times.

Guinea

IT WAS THE FIRST TIME my son (seven years) and daughter (five years) would be attending the same school in Conakry. The French school was about 20 kilometres away from our residence but the traffic was dreadful; a 15 minute ride would last up to two hours, or even three hours, on a bad day. As a result of these long drives, many children were dropped off by drivers and nannies. Some drivers were obliged to wait up to six hours at the school until the children were out lest they would be stuck in traffic and miss the school pick-up hours.

Considered to have a better education standard than most local schools, the French school was where most of the affluent people, government officials and Ministers chose to send their children, many of whom were escorted by personal bodyguards.

It was rare to encounter parents at the school save for the school meetings or special school fêtes and sports tournaments. It is no wonder that I only met and interacted with a few school parents, one of whom was a Guinean mum, her son and mine were best friends. Most Guineans formed closed social bonds among themselves that were difficult to break into. I did meet a few school parents though, mostly foreigners within the expat community; From Somalia, Burundi, Burkina Faso, Senegal, Martinique, Mali, France, Spain, Vietnam and fellow Ugandans among others.

Comoros Islands

IN MORONI, Comoros Islands, I was a little concerned about how my son would handle a new school, a new country, in a rather challenging class and away from his old friends. We arrived a week after "La Rentrée" – the start of the school year. It was just at the peak of the COVID-19 pandemic when almost six months prior, schools had been shut down and home-schooling was the norm. The school was rather small – much smaller than the previous French Schools they previously attended – with slightly over 450 children in primary and secondary school combined. On that first day of school, we dealt with all the usual procedures, had a quick chat with the Director and the teachers who were all seemingly nice and welcoming, and saw our two children off to their individual classes.

Our son had just completed primary level in the previous country and was starting 'Collège' – the equivalent of secondary school in the British school system. My daughter was in CM1 (equivalent of 4th grade). The hours seemed to drag that day as I waited to hear the details of their first day at school, especially from my son. I had the least worries for my daughter; she will quickly integrate as long as she is surrounded by girls within her age bracket. My son too was not exactly the reserved type, so I was confident he would eventually integrate but he had developed a very close friendship with one of his classmates in our previous 'home' in Guinea. I was concerned the absence of his best friend would affect his integration into the new school. I had earlier read somewhere that because they are heavily reliant on their close friends, separating children aged between 10 years and 15 years from their close social circle is likely to cause Expat Child Syndrome (ECP).

At 4 pm that day, I was in the school parking lot anxiously waiting for my son to exit. He stepped out the school gate and spotted me in the distance. With my heart racing, I waved at him and he waved back and gave me a warm smile. My heart melted; *if only I could hug him*. But I knew that was non-negotiable. You see, back when he was eight years old, we made an agreement.

"Maman, can you not hug, kiss or hold my hand when I am at school or around my friends?" he beseeched me. "You can only do this when we are at home".

"Deal", I replied.

Regardless of the urge to grab him and smother him with kisses, this was certainly not the moment to breach that agreement. I cautiously asked him how school went, to which he shrugged and said, "OK".

Well, 'OK' was better than 'bad', right?

To fully integrate them in their new environment, we got them involved in after-school activities like tennis, swimming and creative art classes and organised regular playgroups with their friends.

Most children under a certain age are generally adaptable to new environments – of course there are some younger children that undergo stressful experiences while transitioning from countries and schools. It's usually a lot more challenging for teenagers. Depending on each individual child and family circumstances, I am convinced that the benefits for children living abroad are far more positive than the challenges. Our children have constantly been thrown out of their comfort zones and confronted with uncertainties but have over the years become adaptable human beings. They have learned to accept the pleasant and unpleasant changes, to navigate the unknown, and to respond to their new environments – the journey has not always been easy but has built their character and resilience.

If you are brave enough to say goodbye, life will reward you with a new hello.

— PAULO COELHO

6

"I'LL KEEP IN TOUCH, I PROMISE"

THE FRIENDSHIPS WE MAKE

You may think that life as an expat spouse is a social whirl of lunches, private house parties, cocktails, barbecue weekends and more. Well, you would be right – to an extent. But these 'perks' also come with a lot of challenges, turmoil, and loneliness. Constantly being away from family and old friends, with no support system in the vicinity can be a bummer. But the one thing that is balm to our nomadic souls is the friendships we make wherever we go.

These friendships are often intense and fun but they are also a continuous rotation of hellos and goodbyes that leave us dizzy. Learning and accepting those 'goodbye' moments has been one of the hardest realities to face as expats. The frequency that families have to move to other countries leaves you questioning whether it's even worth saying 'hello' to new families. It makes you wonder whether you are better off as a recluse and just wait out your (usually four-year) work posting before moving onto the next country – and pressing 'repeat'. That way, nobody is emotionally attached to anyone and no huge amount of time is wasted on friendships.

But alas, life doesn't work that way, does it? For some yes, but for many not. So we try over and over again. We move to new countries, settle in, go out, discover places and meet new people. We herd together with them, in surroundings and cultures we barely know. We laugh, cry and complain (a.k.a 'bitch') about the same things. We nurture and hold onto each other so tightly that we impulsively develop whimsical convictions that these friendships will last past the end of the work posting. When we leave and move to another country, we usually waffle on, amidst genuine sadness, about how we will call each other twice or ten times a day.

Some of these friendships have endured and we treasure them. However, many have organically drifted away and we've had to let go and that is OK. But it would take a big part of this book away if we failed to acknowledge the people with whom we've shared many laughs, meals, fears and concerns plus those that have lent us their ears and warmly welcomed us into their homes.

Our lives are richer because of every single person we have encountered along the way.

Julie
Zimbabwe

ALL MY LIFE, I have been blessed with a wonderful family of friends, but making new friends from scratch requires energy, time and intentional effort. On work postings abroad, I have always felt like the 'new kid' during those first months before I can comfortably say I have found 'my tribe'. Some of those relationships have blossomed into lifetime friendships.

Even though we eventually expanded our social circle, the first six months in Harare were a little isolating. As is often the case, expats tend to make friends with fellow expats (perhaps because they have a natural feeling of solidarity and understanding of how isolating the expat world can be) but Zimbabwe was special because at least ninety-five percent of our friends were Zimbabwean nationals.

Our first friends in Harare were Susan and her husband Fred. We clicked the first time we met, there was never a dull moment with this duo. Susan is down to earth with a refreshing sense of humour (she is one of those that don't sweat the small stuff) and a fun approach to life. Eighteen years later, she remains as funny as ever and is seemingly ageless (share the secret girl!).

We made wonderful acquaintances via Susan and Fred. Among them is Vivienne. She is passionate about Zimbabwean artefacts particularly Shona stone sculptures and together with her team of skilled artists, they create magnificent stone sculptures. Displayed in her garden were outstanding sculptures towering at over two metres. Viv's French husband and his brother are top chefs and wine connoisseurs. Thanks to them, they tantalised our taste buds with *Haute Cuisine* and wine tasting shindigs over chats and hearty laughs. We shared various memorable moments with Sandy, Emma, Sonia, Angolan Bella and other fantastic people.

Moira was hubby's colleague. She thoughtfully and graciously welcomed and helped us settle in our new environment during the first few weeks of our arrival in Harare.

I met Karen in our French Class at Alliance Française. With her glistening smile (I hardly saw her in a bad mood), she was approachable with an amiable demeanour to her. Our French sucked at the time and we laughed at each other when we attempted to speak or read a sentence out loud in French.

There is always that one crazy-in-a-good-way friend, and that was Cameroonian Jane. She regularly organised 'dance-lunches' (is that even a word?) in her home where we savoured delicious Cameroonian dishes and danced the afternoon away to all kinds of *Lingala* (Congolese) songs. There was no excuse not to dance *chez elle*, she didn't care whether you had two left feet or no booty; you had to shake whatever your mama gave you.

The ongoing economic crisis impacted the entertainment industry in 'Zim' but lack of entertainment venues didn't stop us from creating our own 'happiness' – nothing will stop a Zimbabwean from having a good time. The fun times were mostly at private social gatherings (house parties) and for a change of scenery, we occasionally dropped by at this dingy bar/restaurant with friends. It was the only one-stop 'happening' place to eat out, karaoke and dance. It was balmy dim lit, you could hardly see your neighbour's face nor the food on your plate. Humour, sympathy and *lotsa* wine got us through most of the economic tough times and we formed a tight support network. You can't argue with that sort of intensity.

WITH AN ENDLESS ARRAY of entertainment and leisure opportunities, the city of Johannesburg is vibrant and I assumed making South African friends would be easy peasy but the reverse was true. Even though South Africans are naturally approachable people and will effortlessly strike up a conversation with a stranger, I didn't make solid acquaintances that exceeded casual conversations.

There was however one exception. I met South African Cisca at a modelling photoshoot we did together and we struck up a conversation immediately. She is poised, calm and cool. Even if we hardly saw each other physically, we stayed in touch. When she was not riding her Harley-Davidson Roadster, she was travelling to Chicago for work (every other two weeks to be exact). At first, I admired her ability to travel frequently (I turned a deaf ear when she said it was not as fun as I thought) but eventually realised it was not my cuppa tea – especially not with my motion sickness issues. And to imagine I once wanted to be an air hostess.

Prior to our move to South Africa, a mutual friend introduced us to Kenyan Esther who lives in Jo'burg (to this day). Compassionate, hospitable and selfless, she always goes the extra mile for the people she loves. I treasure our Eat, Pray, Love moments. We attended church and fellowshipped together, she was my spiritual sister with whom I shared many bonding moments. She was beside my mum in the hospital lobby that night my son was born.

Cameroonian Gigi is dynamic, enthusiastic and compassionate. Eager to support good causes, she is a visionary and friend that brings everybody together. I met a cheerful bunch of people through the monthly soirées she organised.

We carry many fond memories of South Africa. The

ambiance was socially favourable and we had a marvellous time with wonderful people. With a wide variety of restaurants, we enjoyed mouth-watering exotic foods, participated in cultural events, jazz nights and lots and lots of braais in our, as well as, our friends' backyards.

Madagascar

MADAGASCAR was the first French speaking country outside France that I lived in. Being English speaking, I subconsciously gravitate toward making English-speaking friends but the chances of doing that here were very slim since 99.9% of my interactions were with French-speaking people. I wondered how I would survive this 'gendered' language without mixing everything up (*Masculin et Féminin? Mais pourquoi?*).

I was left with two choices; to avoid French-speaking people (which was everybody really) or take the bull by the horns and gamble my way into speaking the French I had neatly stored in my brain. My 'training' started right at home with our house help and Malagasy friends. In time, my confidence levels rose and I could communicate, albeit with a lot of verbal or grammatical mistakes of course that they corrected with kindness and affection which helped a lot.

French Sly was my husband's colleague and our first contact. She is lovely with such a bubbly personality and showed me all corners of Tana. She was the go-to person for finding genuine street shops with quality precious and semi-precious jewellery, art and *all things Malagasy!*

Most of my Malagasy friends were my regular work-out and Zumba dance buddies. Our weekly rendezvous was at the gym on weekdays and girls' nights out on some weekends.

Alice, the social butterfly from Congo and Malagasy Nina were one of my gym classmates I grew fond of. We encouraged and pushed each other during the work-outs. Like me, Nina had a weakness for fried sweet plantains *(hello calories!)*. Lisa from Madagascar introduced me to a sewing class that made me discover a hobby I never knew I would love.

My Malagasy and foreigner friends were a fun and jovial crowd. Kenyan Aileen, my 'designated' dance partner, is witty, with an easy-going character, an endless energy and killer dance moves. If the expression *dance like nobody is watching* was a person, it would be her! I admired her ability to dance to all genres of songs (respect Aileen), it didn't matter if she was with someone or solo on the dance floor, she just danced. Luckily for us (her friends), we were always sure to have her as a partner on the dance floor on our nights out. She is good company and a great cook too. My favourite dish from her kitchen was her home-made Thai food. Yummy!

Sailifa from Mozambique is another friend I hold so dear to my heart. Our children were in the same school but our immediate bond was our love for exercise. She is a well of inspiration and that friend who challenges you to be better. Don't even try to reason with her if you don't have your facts in order, ha! Thanks to her encouragement, she motivated me to jump-start my small business when we relocated to Guinea. Together we enjoyed Zumba and yoga classes. She introduced me to my first yoga experience when I accompanied her to a session. I couldn't stop myself from yawning during that class and the hour seemed to drag. In between the 'downward facing dogs' and trying not to topple over, I just wanted things to end! *This is so boring,* I thought to myself. Much to my surprise, my viewpoint changed towards the end of the session when we lay on the mat for 'Savasana'. I may have been so relaxed that I fell into a sweet slumber. The following morning, I woke up well-rested and feeling good albeit slightly sore (in a good way) in areas of my body I never thought existed. Namaste!

Sailifa, Aileen, Tanzanian Vanessa (whose son and mine were very good friends) and Caroline from Burkina Faso (her daughter and mine were in the same class and were best friends too) were my English-speaking mates in Madagascar. We shared enriching conversations over many lunches and outings, talked about all things and nothing and fantasised about our dreams and life goals.

I met four Aichas; two from Guinea, one from Ivory Coast and another from Senegal. They were my first West African encounters and boy did I love their energy and strong characters. The 'Aicha's' from Senegal and Guinea shared my love for discovering and exploring artisan markets and we bonded over visits to downtown markets in search of good finds.

Guinea

AS AN EAST AFRICAN, my curiosity to live and interact with West Africans became reality when we moved to Conakry. Funny then that the first person I met there was Zambian Christine. A few weeks after our arrival, I was having my nails done at a salon when a lady walked in and without the slightest hesitation, addressed the receptionist in English (remember that Guinea is French speaking). After a few exchanges with the receptionist who was clearly having trouble understanding her, I politely interrupted and translated. I saw the relief on Christine's face, she seemed to be glad someone spoke English. We automatically became buddies.

Unlike our previous postings in (Zimbabwe and Madagascar), most of my friends here were expats. I connected with

Somalian Huda in the parent's waiting area of the French School where we often chatted as we waited for the school bell to go off. She is a kind and beautiful soul. We spent quiet evenings together watching golden sunsets on her balcony that overlooked the ocean, nibbling on snacks and drinking red wine.

American PattiJoy and I met at a mutual friend's house just a few months before she relocated to another country but our friendship grew deep within those few months. I like her sweet and high-spirited nature. She and I practised yoga and we occasionally went out for lunches. I also developed friendships with other yogis in the class and I thoroughly enjoyed our weekend yoga retreats to the neighbouring islands.

Life would be boring without friends that create a gratifying ambiance and atmosphere. Amongst them is Senegalese Cécilia, she was the life of the party and often indulged us in her delicious *Tiep bou diène* and *poulet Yassa* (traditional Senegalese dishes).

Rwandese Mila, is soft-spoken, easy-going and was the coalition builder in our circle of friends. She always brought people together to share wonderful moments at her home.

Fatima from Burkina Faso is that 'morale booster' friend. She is very kind, calm and collected with an unwavering positive attitude. She is never short of compliments and thoughtful words for others and thinks I am an inspiration. Her kind words are always humbling; I think the same of her.

Lovely and kind Haby is one of my few Guinean friends, her son and mine were best friends and got on like a house on fire. Some of hubby's colleagues developed into friendships that surpassed the workplace. Even though we have all been long gone from Guinea, we still link up and spend some holidays together. One of those adorable friends is Safia. She is a social butterfly with countless friends but will treat you like you are the only one. I wonder how she does that.

I WAS thrilled to find fellow Ugandans in Conakry (the entire Ugandan community composed of five people, me included). Maria and May were my Ugandan sisters. Every time we got together, they awakened the Ugandan spirit in me. We chatted in Luganda (which is the most widely spoken language in Uganda), laughed, danced to our local songs, ate 'matooke' (green plantain), and 'Rolex'(not the watch but rather a popular food item in Uganda combining an omelette and vegetables wrapped in a chapati).

Binette from Guinea, a fashion model and Aminata are two lovely sisters with a passion for fashion and a fashion house. They host the 'Guinea Fashion Week' every year and honoured my brand with an invitation to participate at their fashion shows. They are driven, enterprising and inspirational.

Eléne from Martinique was, like me, a member of 'Conakry Accueil' Association. She was an active member with a benevolent attitude and extended her kindness and dynamism to everyone she crossed paths with. She and her husband were natural-born hosts who opened their home to everybody. In the years that ensued, she voluntarily organised numerous social gatherings; school events, Kids' Easter parties and festive Christmas parties with a Martiniquais flavour. We participated in various projects together and I appreciated her good cheer. What struck me most about her was the manner in which she immaculately performed every project she spearheaded. Whatever she did was down to a T. In her words, *il vaut mieux ne rien faire du tout que mal faire quelque chose (*in otherwords, it's better to do nothing at all than to do it half baked*)*. Oh, she made the most delicious upside-down pineapple cake too. She shared her recipe with me but mine isn't as delectable as hers.

Some relationships stretch beyond the dimensions of friendships and into deeper connections. Burundian KCD arrived in Conakry a year after us. She was introduced to me by my best friend Aude. Our children were in the same school and get along well together. She's got a sparkling personality, a heart of gold and a strong sense of family. She's got an undeniable love for children and was always the favourite 'Auntie' for all the children whose lives she touched. She went to great lengths to organise super-duper playdates for the children at her home and managed to make the other parents look bad (thank you KCD, ha!). She spared nothing to delight everyone with fun activities and together we shared beautiful memories. Our families occasionally meet up during holidays and it's always a pleasure to reconnect.

Comoros Islands

AT THE TIME OF PUBLISHING this book, we will have been a year and half in our current relocation in the Comoros Islands. I joined 'Moroni Accueil' Association immediately after our arrival and my family and I were warmly welcomed with open arms by its members. Our first weekend was a nature walk with a friendly group of ladies from the association. We hiked through dense vegetation, admired the colourful bougainvillea flowers and views then stopped at our hosts' home where we were treated to snacks, sipped on fresh coconut water from the shell and made acquaintance with other members.

Most Comorians are generally friendly with a welcoming spirit. We encountered amazing people who graciously invited us to private gatherings. However, being a small city with a minimal expat community and a limited choice of socialising spots, it was inevitable to always bump into the same faces.

Before our arrival, Sitti from Comoros was introduced to us by Yve who regrettably relocated the same year we arrived on the island. Yve is a wonderful and resourceful soul who graciously provided us information prior to our move to Comoros. Sitti and our children attend the French school and she's become like a sister. She has a pleasing temperament, a gentle nature and is a reliable friend. She and her husband who is Mauritian, enjoy entertaining and often create fun activities surrounded by great company. Through them, we've met a lovely bunch of people with whom we occasionally plan weekend beach trips where we picnic, eat grilled lobster and sweet potatoes under a large Baobab tree that's located a few metres from the beach, accompanied by music and dancing sometimes. I love the simplicity of these outings. The beaches are usually secluded and we, the adults and the children always have a swell of a time.

I HAVE BEEN VERY FORTUNATE to meet and connect with people from all walks of life and from diverse backgrounds, some relationships have turned into great friendships but this chapter wouldn't be complete without recognising and acknowledging the friendships I cultivated before my adventures; friendships that have for over two decades stood the taste of time and distance.

I treasure all my Ugandan girlfriends (those in Uganda and others who've relocated to faraway lands), and my siblings (Joan, Salome, Elizabeth, Andrew, Gabriel ...) who encourage me and bring out the silly in me. We may not always be in touch but when we do, our souls quickly reconnect and we quickly pick up where we left off.

Aude from Burundi has been my friend for as long as I can remember. She defines friendship and has been my greatest teacher on the true meaning of friendship. Our bond dates back to our college years in Uganda and we've been inseparable since. I don't know anybody with baskets full of love, patience and grace for others. Together with her husband Raymond and their children, they readily open their hearts to people. With her, we've shared many pivotal moments, we laugh so hard about absolutely nothing, we cry together and are elated for each other. She understands me even when I say nothing, keeps me grounded and is my greatest cheerleader.

One day I received an unexpected call from 'The Miss Uganda Organisation' congratulating me for being a selected candidate for an audition. I was confused. Thinking it was a mistake, I brushed it off. It turned out that 'sneaky' Aude had secretly registered my name and details for the ongoing Miss Uganda pageant 2001 scouting. That year, after a series of auditions and a month's boot camp of training with the other contestants, I was crowned Miss Uganda 1st Runner Up at one of the most celebrated events in Uganda.

I will forever treasure our friendship. Besides, I cannot get rid of her because she knows too many of my secrets. She is my *don't worry, we'll bury the body and move to the Himalayas together* type of friend, ha!

Amongst my long-term friends is co-author of this book, Pearl. Our friendship dates back to our modelling days, two decades ago when we were skinny (*she still is btw*) with no kids (haha). Our bond has even gotten stronger during the course of writing. She inspired and propelled me to tread unknown paths and turned me into a storyteller (who knew!). Thanks to her, I have been able to reflect, revisit and tell my journey stories. She is a beautiful soul with an always-cheerful persona, it's been an absolute delight working with her on this book. Oh, I enjoy reading her writing, she is one heck of a storyteller!

My old friendships moulded and guided the trajectory of all the relationships I have created in this expat journey. And along the way, I have learnt valuable lessons and feel blessed to have global connections. Besides, what's not to like about having global friends? This way, you are able to visit them, discover a new country and have free accommodation. Now, that's a friendship bargain (wink).

I celebrate the gift of life, love and friendship. Friends are the family you choose.

Pearl
Bangladesh

MY HUSBAND'S COLLEAGUE introduced us to the Dutch club shortly after our arrival in Dhaka, Bangladesh. Within a matter of weeks, it became clear that the club, as well as the numerous other expat clubs would be our homes away from home. It was also in these clubs that we met many of the people in our social circle.

In the Nordic club is where I first met the only Ugandan girl I knew in Dhaka. Bandi walked – or rather waltzed – into the club one afternoon, swaying in sky-high heels and with hair that was braided so long it went until the small of her back. That was the first clue that she was new in Dhaka because one of the challenges I had in Bangladesh was finding someone who could braid my African hair. Naturally I was curious to know where she had got hers braided so I approached her. I immediately picked up on the accent which had an East African strum to it. When we both realised we were from Uganda, we shrieked and hugged in pure delight. She had arrived in Dhaka only a few weeks prior and was understandably feeling overwhelmed with a lot of things. At the time, I was already living in Dhaka for a year and I considered myself the best 'pro' to show her around. We went apartment hunting with her and I introduced her, her husband Tom and their daughter to the (all important) expat clubs. Soft-spoken and always wearing a smile, she is one of the smartest and most chilled-out people I know; not many things phase her.

I am a sucker for intelligent people (I am married to one). So, when Bandi introduced me to Cynthia on a night out, we got on immediately. She is a brilliant, independent and fun

Aussie/Kenyan who was in Dhaka for work. She later introduced me and Bandi to South African Thebogo. All together, we became a pose, exploring and navigating the many delights and challenges of living in Dhaka and she remains a dear friend to this day.

Where German Silvia and her Belgian husband Johan were sitting was where you'd most likely find us too – which was often in the Dutch club. Their son and our oldest daughter attended PreK 3, PreK 4 and Dutch class together and are still thick as thieves. We shared many dinners, drinks, parties, coffees, cigarettes and karaoke nights. They remain ingrained in our lives and we meet up almost every time we are all in Europe.

Dutch Rudy and his Bhutanese wife Shakila are another wonderful couple we met in Dhaka and are still dear friends to this day. Shakila seemed to know a lot of people in Dhaka. She introduced me to many of the school parents, among whom was Sri Lankan Anju, Russian Tanya and her Swiss husband Sirocco as well as Bangladeshi Michelle. Michelle is an extremely down to earth business woman and together with her husband was one of the best hosts in Dhaka, opening their home to guests every couple of months for the best food, drinks and music.

We met New Zealanders Fleur and her husband Paul through our daughters who were best friends in pre-Kindergarten. A few days after meeting, Fleur and I decided to take our two girls for ice cream in one of the restaurants in the city. On arrival, the security guard at the door stopped us in our tracks and sternly informed us that everyone else could go inside – except me. Why? Because I am black. Yep, he actually said that. "Blacks are not welcome here", he firmly repeated. That hit me like a blow and I was beyond astounded. I started walking away, lost for words. Fleur, seething with rage and anger pulled me back, told me not to go anywhere and in her cute New Zealander 'speak', she gave the plonk a mouthful and demanded to see the manager. When the manager came out, he actually tried to explain this bigotry, saying that the reason he had come up with the 'no-blacks-allowed' rule was because of an incident he had had with two black men earlier on. Imagine crucifying an entire race because of an incident with people who happened to be black. He offered us free food as a way of saying 'sorry'. Needless to say, we told him to shove the food in the security guard's *where-the-sun-don't-shine* parts – and drove off.

This thankfully turned out to be an isolated incident in Dhaka and I never experienced this or any other type of racism afterwards. This incident was also the beginning of my friendship with Fleur – not because she had defended me but because I just couldn't get enough of her accent, haha.

We met Dutch Roger and American Carey in the Dutch club (where else) and it was 'like' at first sight. Both are as smart as a whip, have positive vibes and are lots of fun to be around. We shared a love for tennis so we quickly got along. Carey and I were pure amateurs while our other halves had played competitive tennis in their youth. Before long we were swept up in the game, playing for hours, only pausing to gulp glasses of water – or beer. Later in the year, we managed to compete in the inter-club tennis championships (Carey and I in the 'C' level rankings of course).

Italians Eros and Michela as well as South Africans Jude and William often joined in the tennis, dinner and drinks fun most weekends. Left-handed Michela has one of the most beautiful topspin forehands. Off-court, she, Eros and their two children were wonderful hosts who loved to create fun activities for both the kids and adults.

South Korean Kim is like all South Koreans I have met –

beautiful, down to earth and so hilarious. We met at our daughters' school and spent many afternoons in the International club swimming and eating (a lot of) *Dal Makhani*, butter chicken and *Matar Paneer* while the kids played (the kids ate too, at some point). She was one of the people I missed the most when we unexpectedly couldn't return to Dhaka in 2016.

French Emilie and I shared great times from the moment she arrived in Dhaka. She worked for an international NGO and was often away from the city centre so we didn't see each other for most of the week but when she was in town, we spent great evenings doing what we did best in Dhaka – socialising.

I met Thai Jane through Shakila and although it was just a few months before we left Dhaka, she was a beautiful kind soul who often invited us to her house for the most wonderful Thai food, playdates for the kids as well as some free pilates classes for her friends. This girl is the fittest person I know. Oh, and her tennis is incredibly good too.

I spent a lot of mornings in the Dutch club meeting room buried in books, reading for a degree. Dutch Harold, the club manager, was always one of the first people I saw. He thought I was the best thing since sliced bread (haha) and the feeling was mutual. He, the rest of the Dutch Club staff and other club members we socialised with were always incredibly welcoming and I miss them all so much.

China

ARRIVING IN ANY NEW PLACE without a social circle or support network can be nerve racking. One would think that the bigger the city or the more expats there are in a city, the easier it is to meet people. In fact, the opposite is true. Smaller cities tend to have limited choices of restaurants and supermarkets so most expats tend to frequent these same spots thereby bumping into each other and easily forming friendships. Larger cities on the other hand have a lot of choice and just like kids with too many toys, people don't fully explore one place before quickly moving onto the next, newer, shinier one.

Beijing simply had too many restaurants, way too many expats and too many 'first meetings' so trying to create and keep friendships in a ginormous metropolis like Beijing was a challenge that was further compounded by the language barrier. There were of course those 'favourite toys' that we cherished.

Trinidadians Alyssa and Stephen are legends in our books and they made our time in Beijing unforgettable. We met in church – church being a large hall inside the Canadian Embassy in Beijing where our children were starting lessons for receiving the first Holy Communion. We got on immediately and spent so many fun 'liming' weekends together. During this time, I discovered I was pregnant with our second baby. My husband and I decided I'd have the baby back in Europe and so, on a summer evening in June 2019, we went out for pizza with them and said our *see you later, have a great summer* and *it's only six months you know, time goes so fast, so we'll see you back here soon*. Our oldest daughter and I spent the next six months in Europe with my husband subsequently joining us that November for the birth. In January 2020, with a six-week old baby and bags of excitement about returning to our 'normalcy', we travelled back to Beijing. We were also very excited to see Stephen, Alyssa and their two wonderful boys and to resume our 'liming' – with pram, diapers and baby in tow this time. They were the first to visit the new baby. I'm so glad I got to see them then because, only a week after they visited, COVID-19 hit China and we went into lockdown. Three weeks later, with infections running amok, we had to pack up and leave Beijing while they stayed behind. After seven months in Europe, we came back to Beijing ... just two weeks after they had moved back to the Caribbean. I missed them so much.

Like most people we've met, we got to know Americans Andrew and Gabriella through our children at school. Our daughter and theirs started grade 1 in the same class and continued to be assigned to the same homeroom every year, making them close and in turn bringing us the parents close too. They opened up their home so warmly and generously, inviting us to share in many special American holiday traditions, dinners and other fun activities. Their thanksgiving dinners felt like we were with family and their Halloween parties were awesomely American with no decorating and food expenses spared. Through these invitations to their house, we got to meet so many other great people, both expats and locals, one of them being Su-en.

Malaysian Su-en is smart and has an easy aura about her but the best thing about her is her sense of humour – crickets and all (wink wink Su-en ;-)). We also shared commonalities in how we grew up in Malaysia and Uganda respectively. For example; how we used small petrol lanterns when electric power was off, or how in both countries some people don't wear shoes when it rains – they carry them and walk barefoot (shoes are too expensive to be ruined by the rain, you see). She introduced me to the ladies in her tennis group:

Indian Smitha is so sweet, quiet and unassuming. Aletta is from South Africa and she is always, always joyful (she also has the most lethal first serve in our tennis group). American Cindy loves her fitness as much as her tennis. She also made the yummiest bites which she often shared during the tennis breaks. Gabriela and I played together only once before we left

China but she was a great player on court and great company off it. The wonderful South Korean Kara was a dear friend. On court, she amused us with her firebomb energy and her loud, funny exclamations in Korean when she hit or missed the ball. We all met at least twice a week for tennis and occasionally had lunch together (PS, we were less friendly on the tennis court).

Zambian Paddy and I met through a lady from church (you guessed it, that Canadian Embassy hall). From the moment I saw her, I felt like I'd known her for years. A polyglot in training, she articulates her English like she is the Queen's cousin and yet she will go down with the 'African twang' where and when needed, haha. She is kind, down-to-earth, confident, warm, funny and intelligent (I told you I like intelligent friends ;-)). By coincidence, we had a friend in common back in Lusaka because of our stint living in Zambia many years before. We spent many afternoons having lunch and chatting in Beijing, especially when we met in 'mama' Fidele's hair salon. That summer BC (Before COVID), Paddy announced that her husband's job was unexpectedly transferring them to Kuala Lumpur, Malaysia. As much as this was sad for us, there was no stopping our new friendship. We have sometimes spent up to four hours on the phone chatting away. I'm glad the distance hasn't put a damper on our friendship. She's a bonafide sister.

In came another Zambian – Muby. Again, we met in church at the Canadian embassy (this place was like 'Tinder' for friendships). A mother of three who didn't look a day past 30, she is a jovial, free-spirited, straight-talking bomb of fun and barrel of laughter and she made the latter months in Beijing such fun for me. I could call her whenever I needed a shoulder or an ear to unpack some of life's gruelling demands, or when I just felt like putting on my heels, dancing and having a tall, cold drink (usually with a bit of alcohol – don't judge). I miss her.

Jenifer is a no-nonsense but super friendly South African I met on the International Day event at our daughter's school. She is such a laugh but her best quality is her honesty. She tells it as it is and I love her for that. Together with fellow South Africans Phindi, Martha, Nellie, Portia as well as Zambian Eden and Kenyan enigma Mark, we had a lot of fun nights out *Braai'ing* and partying in the 'Jing'.

South Korean Hyeyoon Jung has a heart that matches her looks and personality – warm and so beautiful. Her daughter and mine were in the same class. We had both wanted to meet for a while but Hyeyoon was nervous, thinking that her English wasn't good and that I wouldn't be able to understand her. However, from the first playdate/lunch we had together, I not only understood what she was saying, I was also taken by her sweet nature. I volunteered in the school PTA store at her recommendation and we made sure we got shifts at the same time. A year later when I was in Europe and pregnant with our second daughter, she, her husband and daughter made a trip from London to Belgium just to see me. She was also one of the first people to meet the baby when we finally returned to Beijing after seven months in Europe. We remain in touch to this day.

I met Ecuadorian Veronica in Chinese language class. If there was a near-perfect definition of ageless beauty, this woman is it. She joined the class around two weeks after we had started. She had a fair knowledge of Chinese already so the Chinese teacher asked her to briefly introduce herself. When she mentioned her age, I thought to myself, *well, she may be able to speak a bit of Chinese but she sure doesn't know her numbers in Chinese*. So, I half whispered to her that the number she had just mentioned was '51'. Surely her age had to be HALF that number. “Nope”, she confirmed, “I am indeed 51 years old”. She didn’t look a day past 30. She was always so jovial, upbeat and positive. We bonded over some fun lunches and drinks. Sadly, we were separated for the most part of our stay in Beijing due to COVID-19 but we remain in touch.

In this Chinese class were a few other *laowai* (‘foreigners’) who, like me, were trying to learn Chinese:

American Lisa is soft-spoken (almost careful with her words), zenny (so unbothered by small stuff) and so clearly ‘sharp’. She seemed to whizz through Chinese with ease while the rest of us struggled to read the illegible Chinese hanzi characters – and mind you, she joined the class later than many of us.

Bruno is a calm and collected Brazilian soul (something he either naturally possesses or gets from the yoga philosophy he teaches and practices diligently). Damn good-looking and very personable, it is no surprise he is one of the most sought-after male models and yoga teachers in China.

Meilita comes from Indonesia and she was the baby of the class. Her cute, innocent face was always a happy way of starting the class.

Brazilian Simone had us chuckling on most days because of her absolute inability to pronounce some Chinese words. Granted, Mandarin is hard to learn and speak and we were all struggling, but Simone’s Chinese pronunciations had everyone (including the teacher) doubled up with laughter. She was such a sweet sport though, laughing harder than us through it all. She worked super hard and we were all so impressed with her end of level 1 presentation in front of the class.

While in Beijing, I was a freelance writer with Jing Kids International, the go-to resource for all things Expat, Parenting and international Schooling in Beijing. Here, I worked with an amazing team that included our super funky, cool Managing

Editor Mina Yan. I think because of her super easy-going nature, Mina underestimates how truly genius she is. She is a multitasker who doesn't seem to be fazed by anything. She will simultaneously manage the entire team, a work lunch meeting, reply to everything asked of her with the quickest text or call back and somehow still find time to smile, have fun and be a mother. I love her.

Mina's fellow Americans Cindy and Julie were deputy managing editor and editor respectively. Both are incredibly smart and fun people to be around so, even though we only met a few months before I left China, I still squeezed in fun drinks and nights out with them.

Chinese Fan and I met a week after we moved to Beijing. I was walking around the neighbourhood, trying to soak in everything around me when I saw a Traditional Chinese Medicine (TCM) centre right next to our apartment. I have always loved good acupuncture and a traditional Chinese massage and one of the things that had got me excited about living in China was imagining the endless Chinese massages I would be having. So, I walked into this TCM centre. When Fan greeted me in perfect English and the widest smile, my excitement went through the roof because remember, I was completely lost in translation in China the first few months, so anytime I met someone who was able to speak English, I got super euphoric. Fan was so welcoming and she and I had many yoga sessions in her TCM centre, as well as fun lunches and drinks. We were separated during the months I was in Europe for the birth of our second daughter and during the COVID pandemic.

Alaine is also Chinese and was a manager in one of the coffee shops I frequented near our apartment. From day one, I found her incredibly friendly, lively and easy-going but what impressed me most about her was her freaking brilliant mind. One time she showed me a study plan for a school she was working for. She had just come up with the entire study plan in less than an hour (with coffee and cigarette breaks in between) but it looked like something Albert Einstein would spend a day formulating. I was gobsmacked at this brilliance but she just shrugged – it was absolutely easy-peasy for her. She is also a great piano player, singer and artist and one of the people I love hearing from in China. We keep in touch to this day.

Ruby was introduced to me by my Ugandan friend Margaret who lives in Shanghai. We occasionally met for lunch and enjoyed some incredibly fun nights out. Unfortunately, due to COVID-19, we were separated for most of the time.

Polish Cecylia and I first met in Hong Kong while we were on a family holiday. Her husband worked with mine back in Beijing and we lived in the same residential compound but we had never met until then. Once we got back to Beijing from Hong Kong, we met up for some fun lunches and (bowl) sound healing sessions. Not long after we got back to Beijing, we both found out we were pregnant. We were separated for most of the year 2019 when I went back to Belgium to give birth to our second daughter while she stayed in China. By the time we came back to China in early 2020, she had relocated to Europe with her family. We have shared pregnancy joys, frustrations and everything in between, albeit from a distance. I find her super hilarious and we text each other almost every day.

There are many other social contacts that we treasured; the Church and parent groups at the Canadian Embassy church including the wonderful and hilarious Father Giovanni who cracked us up every Sunday with his hilarious homilies. There was also Grace and Colm who, together with their families gave a lot of their time to help with church services, holy communion teachings and organising many fun-filled Sunday lunches (mmmm, still craving those choco-filled dumplings at Ding Tai Fung).

The ladies at the Champagne and Caviar Club (CCC) Beijing were exquisite. First invited by Gaby, I immediately loved the vibe of the entire group. The group met once a month in different restaurants around Beijing for incredibly amazing and unapologetically glamorous champagne and caviar-filled lunches. It was always, always guaranteed fun for me – with proof in those wobbly walks back home at 4pm.

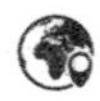

Lebanon

AT THE TIME OF PUBLISHING this book, we were living in Lebanon for less than a year.

British Jessica worked with my husband in Beirut and also lived across the hall from us with her husband David and their two children. We met only two months before they left Beirut but we managed to have some great chats, wines, pizzas, popcorn and fun nights out at the cinema together before they left Lebanon.

Canadian Christine and her family moved to Lebanon a month after we did. Her husband worked with mine and we were introduced pretty quickly. It was one of the easiest and most comfortable first-time meetings – we got along immediately. She is an extremely smart, soft-spoken, hilarious, beautiful, warm and kind mum of two. Did I mention she is smart? Both our families didn't have Christmas plans that year as we had just arrived in Lebanon so she invited us over to theirs for a wonderful Canadian Christmas dinner as well as a New Years' Lebanese meal and drinks. We also enjoyed fun trips outside Beirut as well as lunches, coffee and 'other drinks'.

I met Lebanese Hayat a few weeks after we moved to Beirut. Our daughters were in the same class and she ran the parents' WhatsApp group so she added me to it. She invited our daughter to her house for her first playdate. So warm, generous, kind and *soooooo* beautiful, we hit it off immediately. She knew where to find everything all over Beirut. She was always there when I needed something or had a question about Lebanon.

I treasure the people I've met, some of whom have become friends for life. Weirdos do keep the same company (haha!).

There are no norms. All people are exceptions to the rule that doesn't exist.

— FERNANDO PESSOA

7
DID YOU KNOW?
NORMS, HABITS AND OTHER ODDITIES

Pearl

China

I thought that my home country Uganda – and the African continent in general – had way too many cultural norms, beliefs and idiosyncrasies ... until I moved to China. The similarities are quite eerie too and one of the reasons I loved living in China. Here are a few quirky ones I came across.

Zuo yuezi is the month-long confinement of a new mother. Chinese believe that after child birth, a woman needs at least a month to recover from the torturous journey the body goes through to bring out a child (and they are right – it should in fact be one full year of recovery). During this month of recovery, the new mother is forbidden from showering, washing her hair and going outside. She is instructed to stay in bed as much as possible and only hold the baby when breastfeeding. She wears long sleeved shirts, long pants and socks, is fed lots of chicken or fish soup with no salt and is not allowed to watch TV, read books or stay near an air conditioning unit. *Zuo Yuezi* has some similarities with how new mothers are cared for in Uganda and had I given birth to my daughters in Africa or China, I would have welcomed this pampering with no complaint – apart from the month-long shower ban.

Chinese believe that when a baby is born, he/she is already one year old. They don't believe in zero months or years. Oh, and after the Chinese New Year, they add another year to your age. So, our second daughter was born in November which made her one year already. Then came Chinese New Year three months later in February the following year and she suddenly, magically, Chinese-ly, turned two years old. Go figure!

When babies spend their first 100 days on earth, it's a BIG deal, not only in China but across most of Asia. The celebrations are like wedding parties. This is when all relatives and friends can finally come to meet the baby.

Chinese have a very popular delicacy known locally as *pi dan* 皮蛋 or 'the Century Egg'. It is basically a duck egg that looks rotten and ready to throw away. But throw it away they don't. To turn a normal egg into 'pi dan', it is first wrapped in a mixture of ash, clay, salt and straw before it is dipped in lye and stored away. After about a month, it is unwrapped to reveal an egg white that is now a translucent brown colour and a gooey yolk that is now a blueish, greyish, rotten-ish colour with an overpowering smell of sulphur and ammonia. During famous Chinese festivals like the Dragon Boat Festival, this egg is a popular gift to friends and relatives. *Ni xiang cháng chang ma?* (Do you want to taste?) Ahhh, no, thanks.

In China, just like in Africa, looking someone in the eye and holding their gaze while they speak is considered too direct. In Africa for example, when an adult is reprimanding a child and that child looks straight up and directly into an adult's eyes, the village elders will be summoned immediately to discuss the *mugweenyufu* child who *cannot humbly look down to the ground when I'm talking to him.*

Chinese women and men don't celebrate their 30th and 40th birthdays respectively. These ages are considered to be dangerous and precarious years in one's life so, many will jump right from being 29/39 years old to 31/41 years old. The 33rd and 66th birthdays aren't enthused about much either. To ward off the supposed evil spirits attached to these birthday numbers, several rituals are performed and one of them involves chopping a piece of meat 33 times or 66 times. Surely, no evil spirit can survive that number of chops.

Staying with numbers, the number '4' is to Chinese what 'triple 6' is to most of us – it is considered to be a very unlucky number. On the other hand, the numbers '6' and '8' are very lucky numbers in China. People spend a fortune incorporating the number 8 into their everyday lives; from their car plates to living on the eighth floor. The number '38' is also not favoured much because when you say each number separately – sān and bā – it means 'bitchy'. Incidentally, International Women's day falls on March 8, which is 3/8 if you write it the American or Chinese way. *Happy San Ba day, B*****s. :-)*

Chinese don't open gifts in front of guests. So, don't be offended when your gift is placed on the side and opened after you leave. I must say, I'm with the Chinese on this one too. I never understood why people have to open gifts immediately after they are given them. I remember my first Christmas in Europe. My father-in-law gave me a gift. I said my polite 'thank you' and lay it down next to me ... until I realised everyone was looking at me and waiting for me to open it. In Africa, just like in China, you keep gifts wrapped until everyone goes away. The joy (or disappointment) of seeing what gift you got is for you and only you.

Chinese are obsessed with keeping their feet and legs warm. My Ayi (housekeeper) freaked out every time she saw me and my children without socks or wearing shorts or sleeveless shirts even in the middle of the summer. Many Chinese wear socks all year round, in open-toe sandals, in closed shoes or in scorching hot weather. They believe that colds, body aches, joint pains and headaches all come from having cold feet and legs. I grudgingly started wearing them more around the house, but you won't catch me wearing them with sandals and certainly not during the hot summer days.

When one comes down with a cold or flu-like symptoms, Chinese have no shortage of concoctions for cure; some herbal and some with a modern twist. One day, I got a sore throat, a bad cough and developed a high fever. After slightly reprimanding me for not listening to her *wear socks at all times* advice, my Ayi rushed off on her scooter and was back a few minutes later, laden with a 2-litre bottle of Coca Cola, brown sugar (Hong Tang), cane sugar cubes that looked like ice cubes, pears, ginger, and what looked like lemongrass. She made me two drinks; the first one had the pears and ice-cube sugar boiled together in water. For 'medicine' number two which was for my sore throat, she melted *aloooooot* of the brown sugar, added the full 2 litres of Coca Cola and when this mixture was fiercely bubbling on the stove, she added *aloooooot* of ginger. She then offered me a boiling hot cup of the mixture and insisted I drink it quickly. I couldn't even blow off some steam from the cup to cool it down slightly.

I can report that these cures worked like magic. My husband and oldest daughter who had both caught the flu tried these concoctions too. Our coughs and fevers disappeared after only a day of taking this. But boy did our calorie count hit the roof with all that sugar.

Chinese don't like sitting on the floor. This is a divergence from their similarities with Africa where people gladly sit on the floor to eat, play or even sleep. Chinese people rather squat than sit on the floor.

The spitting. We've already extensively covered this but it's still worth mentioning. It's common for your driver to momentarily stop the car, clear his throat, open the door and chuck his phlegm out on the road. And that's a good driver, because others will just open the window and spit out while still driving. I never sit behind the driver for fear that this spit could make a U-turn with the wind and come flying back in the car and hit me in the face.

Chinese drink a lot of tea as well as hot or warm water often flavoured with small pieces of lemon, carrots, cucumber or ginger. In many restaurants, the first thing they will offer you before you order a meal is a glass of hot water. I'm now a hot water convert and even on scorching hot days, I drink warm beverages.

In some local restaurants, whole chickens or ducks are weirdly served with their heads and feet still nicely attached. Hmmm, try eating that chicken while it's staring at you. Well, not exactly staring but, cursing you in its resting state.

In most restaurants, appetisers arrive with the main meal. Furthermore, food ordered by several people on one table doesn't arrive at the same time. If you are a group of say, four people, you will all start eating at different times. If you decide to politely wait for the others' order to arrive, you may be waiting a long time. Similarly, the *fu wu yuan* (waiter) will very quickly clear the plates of those that have finished their meal while others are still eating. This we know in the West to be impolite. In China, this is normal.

Chinese people talk loudly. At times, it sounds outright aggressive but that's just how they talk, it's in their culture. In restaurants or on public transport, a phone conversation that's meant to be between two people will be heard by an entire carriage.

When our youngest daughter started sitting upright and could play with toys, our kind housekeeper was always playing with her for hours on end. But there was one problem; she rattled the baby's toys so loudly while repeatedly calling the baby's (Chinese) name. One day, a Chinese friend explained to me that in old China, talking or rattling things loudly next to a baby was one way of finding out if the child was deaf or not. This was new China, so I kindly asked her to take it down a notch.

Staying with loud noises, Chinese slurp loudly and excessively while eating, especially when consuming their soup. Apparently, it's because they eat it while it's still very hot, so the slurping is to help cool it down. Not sure that explanation helps my ears.

Ladies don't come first. Senior males come first. So, when entering a building, a male senior will be ushered in first. Similarly, in restaurants, they will be served before ladies.

Chinese people (at least the ones I saw in Beijing) show their wealth but don't show OFF their wealth. I've seen Bugatti's and other six-figure dollar cars driving around Beijing with the driver looking rather 'normal'. I think that they are quite modest for the money-bags that they are. There were some *fuerdai* (second generation rich) that were very 'showy' with their (parent's) wealth. Some reportedly have their pets 'woof-ing' around wearing the latest apple watches and travelling on private jets. Little spoilt beasts (the *fuerdai*, not the pets)

Big earlobes and big noses symbolise luck, happiness and success. So technically, the Baganda people of Uganda – famous for their generous nose sizes – and the Masai people in Kenya with long, pulled earlobes, should be the happiest, most successful and luckiest fellas on earth – gospel according to the Chinese.

In China, the colour red represents good fortune while white and black are for funerals or sickness.

Chinese women keep their maiden name. This was encouraged and promoted years ago by the Communist Party that (rightly) saw women as equal to men and therefore didn't need a man's name to validate them or a marriage (I totally agree).

I have seen some men in China unashamedly holding purses for their women. I've chuckled a bit with this one. I admire their open-mindedness but I'll keep my purse to myself, thank-you-very-much.

Bangladesh

TRAFFIC IN DHAKA is legendary and I've already said enough about it. Being stuck in Dhaka traffic was the only time I cursed like a f******* sailor. I've seen ambulances with patients in urgent need of care, stuck in Dhaka traffic for hours, not moving an inch. I don't ever want to hear anyone complaining about traffic, unless they've once lived in Dhaka.

Given the traffic mess on their roads, Bangladeshis are really chilled-out people. I barely saw anyone expressing anger if a car, rickshaw or an animal blocked them off in traffic. They would simply find that one-inch space still miraculously available between cars, and somehow manoeuvre away from whatever was blocking them. I couldn't believe they were not beating each other up all the time.

Boy or boy do Bangladeshis spit! The spitting starts with what you'd think is a simple innocent clearing of the throat. But, it starts building up in volume and the FINALE is a loud, glottal sound before the sputum is collected in the mouth and, through years of practice I suppose, the person brings the lips together in an oval/round shape, tactfully lets the tongue out for a nanosecond before expertly ejecting the (yellow/green/brown) phlegm with an accurate trajectory to the ground where it rests until the sun burns it to a dry yellow-red spot (or you accidentally step in it). The 'spitter' occasionally follows this up with a loud cough. Years of first or second-hand smoking, coupled with incessant chewing of betel nut as well as the high pollution have all played their part in some serious lung damage to these folks.

If there was ever a 'Staring' sport in the Olympics, Bangladeshis would win every medal. Enough said!

Orderly lines? Queues? What's that? Bangladeshis are 'allergic' to queues. I can't use any other term to describe the phenomenon, for it must be a medical problem – if they made orderly queues they'd probably feel unwell.

Can I take your picture? No? OK, smile ... and flash! Yes, wherever you go in Bangladesh, there is a crowd following you, asking to take a picture and before you answer (usually with a 'No' for me), cameras are already out and people are busy snapping away. At some point, I simply got tired of trying to resist it and so I just smiled widely for their pictures.

"What, who, how, why, where?". Most Bangladeshis are an inquisitive bunch. They do ask a lot of questions. At some point, they may even ask you the name of your mother, father, siblings and your first pet. They want to know EVERYTHING about you.

It's safe to say that universally, a shake of the head from side to side generally means 'no', and shaking of the head up and down will mean a 'yes'. Right? Well, in Bangladesh, it is the direct opposite. 'Yes' is with a little wobble of the head from side to side (while repeating 'yes' about three times for added effect).

Dhaka is one of the most polluted cities in the world (World AQ ranking 2019 – *numero uno*). It's a miracle we came out with our lungs intact. The weird thing is we didn't really 'feel' the pollution when we were there. We largely went about life with no masks and no air filters.

Sheikh Hasina, the prime minister of Bangladesh (when we lived there), is a woman. Her closest political rival – former prime minister and first female president of Bangladesh, Khaleda Zia – is also a woman. Who run the world?? Girls!

Bangladesh has one of the highest prevalence of Dengue fever. After one year of living in Dhaka, we thought we'd escaped it but our daughter got it and had to be admitted to hospital for one week. I've already covered this in Chapter 4. But it's worth mentioning again.

Apart from Ugandans (OK, I may be a bit biassed here), Bangladesh people are some of the friendliest and kindest people that I've met so far. This probably further explains the lack of road rage, despite the fact that they drive like total lunatics. They just tolerate a lot and are so welcoming to everyone.

Asia's longest beach is located in Bangladesh. Cox's Bazar beach runs uninterrupted for 120 kilometres. But don't expect to whip out your bikini and sunbath. The country's mainly Muslim population, although quite secular, is also conservative and they frown upon such beach wear.

I heard – but never witnessed – that young people or wives in Bangladesh have to show respect to the elderly and their husbands respectively by touching their feet. Why the feet? I don't know.

THERE ARE FIVE OR MORE ways of writing a name of a place or city in Lebanon. If you want to go to 'Byblos' but you find yourself in either 'Jbeil', 'Jebeil', 'Jbail', 'Jbayl' or 'Jubayl', relax my friend; it's the same place. 'Batroun' is also written as 'Batrun', 'Bitron', 'Botrys' and 'Lebanon' is written as 'Liban', 'Libnan' or 'Lubnan'.

In Lebanon, you can ski in the morning and swim in the afternoon. No kidding! It only takes you about two hours to drive from Beirut to the Bsharri region, for example. There, you can slip your ski boots on, slide down a crispy snow-capped slope and a few hours later, drive back to Beirut or other coastal cities and swim in the Mediterranean Sea.

There are three main religious groups in Lebanon; Muslims, Christians and the Druze (an Arab esoteric group that does not identify as Muslim). The president of the country is traditionally a Maronite Christian, the prime minister a Sunni Muslim, and the speaker of parliament a Shia Muslim. A Muslim man can marry a non-Muslim girl but a Muslim girl is forbidden from marrying a non-Muslim man. Druze people can never marry outside their community.

Lebanon is a textbook example of how people of different religious backgrounds can coexist peacefully (although this has taken a hit in recent years of turmoil and tensions). Pilgrims departing for Hajj were once blessed by both Muslim and Christian religious figures in the country. In the 70's, Christian leaders had a specially reserved place in St. George Orthodox Cathedral in Tripoli for their Muslim counterparts to sit and watch the Easter proceedings. It is very common for Muslims to put up Christmas decorations as is common for Christians to attend Iftar dinners. Such is the openness and beauty of Lebanese culture.

Staying with religion, Lebanon has the world's first shared holiday by both Christians and Muslims – March 25, the feast of the Annunciation, a dedication for the shared admiration for Mary Virgin Mother of Jesus in both religions.

Continuing with the religious theme (bear with me if you are an atheist), the tomb of Noah (yep, that Noah with the ark) is ALLEGEDLY located in a mosque in Karak Nuh, a village in the Bekaa valley.

Lebanon is in the Middle East but is allegedly not part of Arabia. Confusing? Well, there's some geographical evidence to support this; The Bekaa extension of the Great Rift Valley divides Lebanon from Syria and marks the boundary between two of the Earth's tectonic plates. So, geologically speaking, Lebanon is part of Africa.

Lebanese people love a good nip and tuck. Before the economic situation worsened in Lebanon, Beirut was the plastic surgery capital of the Middle East with folks from neighbouring countries dashing here for a weekend nose-job, face-lift, butt-lift, tummy tuck or even a snip and tuck down the (ahem) *fandango* area. The most popular body parts for Lebanese to retouch are the nose and lips. Walking around with a bandage or plaster on their face post-op is like a medal of valour – it is evidence of your 'improved' self. I've seen people walking around looking like twin versions of Michael Jackson. Why they believe that a smaller nose and gargantuan lips are the definition of beauty is beyond my comprehension. But then again, their money, their bodies ... their fandangos.

Wedding days in Beirut are big and loud affairs. The wedding party drives around the neighbourhood honking car horns, blaring loud music and setting off loud fireworks.

Before these weddings take place however, a woman is still expected to be a virgin (or born-again virgin) on her wedding day. One of the most popular plastic surgery in Lebanon is the hymenoplasty – a procedure done to restore virginity or a veneer of it – hence the 'born-again' virgin. Most of these procedures are done with the utmost discretion because if a man found out that his new wife had already been 'touched', he may choose to divorce her.

Beirut was the first city in the Ottoman Empire to have a girls' school – The American School for Girls, which is now the Lebanese American University.

Unfortunately, allowing girls to attend school does not extend their rights to citizenship matters. A Lebanese man will confer citizenship to his foreign wife and their subsequent children after a year of marriage but a Lebanese woman can never confer the same to her foreign husband and children.

In Lebanon, Christmas is celebrated not once but thrice a year. Christians in Lebanon follow the Gregorian, Armenian and Julian calendars. This means that the Catholics celebrate Christmas on 25 December, the Armenians on 6 January and the Orthodox on 7 January. That's lot of trips for Santa and Rudolph the Reindeer. Imagine his carbon footprint.

Many Lebanese are big on aphrodisiac foods. They use the Moloukhai plant and Sahlab powder in hot drinks to apparently 'warm up' some parts of the anatomy.

Staying with food (but not the one that heats up your 'ahem' regions), Lebanese cuisine is thriving in the world. From Hummus and Tabbouleh that is popular in Europe, North America and Oceania, to Kibbe which is very popular in Brazil, Lebanese have the best food I have ever tasted.

Julie
Zimbabwe

DISCOVERING NEW AND UNUSUAL cultures and customs can knock you for six in the beginning. As you immerse yourself into, and get accustomed to them however, you begin to realise how similar we all are. What we find unconventional about other cultures and customs is actually what has shaped the facets of lives for generations and generations.

At the peak of its infamous inflation in 2008, Zimbabwe issued a 100 trillion Zimbabwean dollar note. At the time, a wheelbarrow load of banknotes could buy you only a loaf of bread or a bag of onions. The country inevitably ditched its own currency, the Zimbabwean dollar, for foreign currency and became a multi-currency nation making it one of the few countries in the world where you can buy an item priced in South African Rands, pay for it in US Dollars and receive change in Euros or the Botswana pula. Go figure!

Zimbabweans are a mix of ethnic groups, majority are the black Zimbabweans of mainly Shona and Ndebele tribe, minority groups include white Zimbabweans (aka Rhodesians) who are mainly of British origin, and Asian ethnic groups of mostly Indian and Chinese. The tribe of the 'Vadoma' people is a small ethnic group in Western Zimbabwe who commonly known as 'Ostrich people' or the 'two-toed tribe'. 25% of the population from this tribe are born with a genetic defect with three of the middle toes missing on their feet. The two outer toes are turned inward giving an ostrich-feet appearance. Since the 'Vadoma' people are forbidden to marry outside their tribe, the defect is passed on from one generation to another.

'Till death do us part'. This part of marriage vows is taken quite literally by some Zimbabweans because over there, marriages (customary or civil) can only be dissolved by death. Divorce, although legal, is seen as shameful and a disgrace and divorcees may be shunned by the local community.

Zimbabwe holds the Guinness World Record (2013) as the country with the highest number of official languages at a national level – 16 official languages in total. Of these, Shona, Ndebele and English are the most commonly used.

Mermaids are not just characters in children's animation stories. In Zimbabwe, there is a strong belief in their existence. But rather than being loved, they are blamed for many unfortunate events such as murder, kidnapping, torture and rape.

While many men all over the world are struggling to shed off that extra fat around the bellies with some paying for expensive surgeries, many Zimbabweans consider large bellies as a sign of success and wealth. The rounder the belly, the wealthier a man is deemed – meat is so expensive you see, so to have a fat belly means you are able to afford meat everyday – to hell with those calories and other health issues.

Similar to my country Uganda, every kind of toothpaste in Zimbabwe is 'Colgate', every soft drink 'Coke', every washing powder 'Omo' and every shoe polish 'Kiwi'. Some brand names stick for life.

South Africa

SOUTH AFRICA is also known as the 'Rainbow Nation' because of the diversity in its peoples. It is a melting pot with people of African, Asian and European descent. The different racial groups are classified as Blacks, Whites, Indians and Coloureds, the latter being a name created by the Apartheid regime to classify people of mixed ancestry.

Each of these groups has its own deep history, culture, beliefs and traditions. In the Zulu culture for instance, one announces his or her arrival to a host's home by shouting loudly from the gate. In Indian homes, it's considered rude to refuse food or drinks offered by a host. This great diversity of cultures also makes for a fusion pot of African, European and spicy Indian cuisines in South Africa.

Despite this distinct cultural diversity, the lasting effects of the apartheid era is still clear for all to see. Some neighbourhoods in South Africa are still separated based on race, leaving a chasm between the White minority and the Black majority in all social levels like education and economic opportunity. Certain Black and Coloured areas tend to have their own schools, clinics, churches separate from the White people areas. Fortunately, South Africa is making steady progress in erasing some of these historic differences with many flourishing in the free climate of the post-apartheid era. Most supposedly 'white areas' are starting to be occupied by the affluent 'Blacks' creating a harmonious group of people.

South Africans, regardless of ethnic group, use a lot of slang in their oral communication. 'Shame' is used as a term of endearment and not always as a word of humiliation. It's used to express sympathy or to mean 'cute', 'adorable' or to sympathise with someone. For instance, if you saw a cute little puppy you would say, "Oh shame, it's so adorable".

The word 'Robots' does not mean those programmable human-like machines; it is another word for 'traffic lights'. So, when someone tells you to "turn right at the robots", don't expect to see that I-Robot in Will Smith's movie before you turn right.

Izzit (*izt*) means 'oh really?', 'is that so?', or 'did you?'. Similarly, the word *Eish* (*Ayshh*) is used to express surprise, disapproval, pity or regret. Lekker (Lekk-irr with a rolling 'r') means 'good' or 'nice'. *Bru* (brah) is a term of affection, shortened to mean 'brother'. *Howzit* means 'how is it going?' So, the next time a local South African says to you, "Eish bru, howzit? We missed you at the braai, shame you didn't make it because we had a lekker time," respond with a confident *Izzit*?

The words *now, now-now* or *just now* are paradoxical terms used by South Africans that leave you truly perplexed. I never really figured these ones out in the 3 years we lived there. *Now* can mean 'eventually', 'maybe' or 'never'. The term *Now-now* on the other hand means 'shortly' (as in, something might actually be done). *Just now* means 'later, not immediately'. This one is risky because you are not sure when something will be done; could be in 10 minutes, in a few hours, or within days.

So, if you ask a local for help and he/she tells you 'now', look for an alternative solution. Or if they say, "We will have dinner 'now', but not 'now now', just know you will be hungry for a while. Confused? Yeah, me too. ;-)

South Africa is the largest meat producer in Africa and consumes meat in plenty too. The typical weekend ritual is the famous *braai* (barbecue) where steaks, chicken, lamb, pork chops, *boerewors* (a spiced sausage) and game meat like springbok, kudu, ostrich and warthog are barbecued and enjoyed. This backyard braai is a communal event for friends and family to converge, chat, be merry and discuss sports and current affairs. When invited to a braai, it's advisable to check first with your host if you need to carry some raw meat to cook. *Biltong* (dried slices of plain or spicy beef) is another delicacy sold in various grocery shops in South Africa.

Staying with their meat, portions in South Africa are quite generous. In certain restaurants, steaks are served by the kilo or if you wish for something smaller you can get yourself a 'lady steak' which is ONLY 450grams. One mid-afternoon hubby and I walked into a Cape Town restaurant for a quick and light snack before a planned dinner later that evening. We chose to share a burger with fries and wash that down with some wine. When the burger arrived, I was gobsmacked at the size of it – it literally could feed a small village. The wine was also generously poured to the brim of the glass. The French could take a leaf out of South Africa's wine book and improve on their wine serving sizes. ;-)

Repeatedly complimenting an object in the home of your South African hosts makes them feel compelled to gift it to you out of politeness. Of course any courteous person would politely decline but I saw some who went ahead and accepted these gifts from their hosts. Not sure I'd say no to a nice 'Monet' or 'Picasso' though ... I mean, I would only compliment it – about one hundred times only – and if someone felt 'compelled' to 'gift' it to me, so be it (haha).

While male circumcision is considered a rite of passage for a young man in many African and other cultures, in South Africa, circumcision is subjected to deviant boys who, according to their parents, are out of control. Kraal men capture the deviant boy and carry out the operation using a sharp blade. It's forbidden for the boy to cry from pain. After the operation, the portion that has been cut has to be buried by the boy on an ant hill to be eaten up by the ants. Not sure what kind of lesson the deviant boy is supposed to learn from this?

Similar to Ugandan culture, South Africans treat their elders with reverence. Older men are respectfully addressed as *Tata* (Xhosa word for father), *Oom* (Afrikaans word for uncle) or sir. Women elders are referred to as *Mama* (Xhosa word for mum) or *Tannie* (Afrikaans word for aunt) or *ma'am* or *Sisi* (sister) for a younger woman.

A friend and I were at a Jo'burg restaurant one fine afternoon and as we were placing our orders, I noticed our waiter's name tag. On it was written 'Perseverance.' For a moment I thought it was a message displayed for the clients – you know, a sort of positive-thinking/motivational message. Turns out South Africans – particularly Black South Africans give some interesting abstract nouns as names to their children. Other examples of such names are: 'Freedom', 'Knowledge', 'Generous', 'Gift', 'Precious', 'Blessing', or 'Inspiration'.

Sport is deeply embedded in all social facets of South Africa and is a conversation starter. South African boasts as the second country after England to host the rugby (1995), soccer (2010) and cricket (2003) World Cups. Soccer and rugby are the two most popular sports. Soccer is more popular with blacks, rugby more popular with whites and cricket has a big Indian following. It's not uncommon for South Africans to watch two matches simultaneously. They will literally switch from one soccer game to another cricket game on TV, or listen to the rugby match commentary on the radio while watching soccer on TV.

'Toyi Toyi' is a South African protest dance used to express grievances. It is a high-intensity dance that involves jogging or jumping with high knees from one foot to another and accompanied by rhythmic chanting or singing. The dance was initially used to protest against white minority rule in the 1980s and employed as a weapon to intimidate the Apartheid state police but it is still used today in celebrations and protests.

South Africa has 11 official languages among which are the popular tongue-clicking Zulu, Xhosa, and Sotho languages. Clicking languages incorporate clicks into a portion of the consonants of the words. The speaker produces a distinctive popping or smacking sound that is created from the tongue and the roof of the mouth. A click may in some cases make up as much as 70% of the spoken language. So interesting.

Table Mountain, located in Cape Town, South Africa, is one of the oldest mountains on the planet – believed to be approximately 360 million years old.

Route 62 is said to be the longest wine route in the world. It spans a distance of 850 kilometres stretching from Cape Town to Port Elizabeth. Sip on that you wine lovers. ;-)

Madagascar

LOCATED SOUTHWEST of the Indian Ocean and off the southeastern coast of Africa, Madagascar is not only a movie (ha!) but the fourth largest Island in the world. It is also known as the Great Red Island due to the reddish tint of its earth. The Malagasy people are descendants of mostly Asian (particularly Indonesian), Arab and African people. In the inner cities of Madagascar are the fair looking people and the darker-skinned people are mostly from the coastal areas. They primarily speak Malagasy (a language with Bantu, Arabic influences) and French.

Contrary to the famous Hollywood movie 'Madagascar' this gigantic island does not have any trace of tigers, lions, zebras, giraffes or hippopotamuses. They however do have lemurs, one of the rarest species in the world (as portrayed by King Julien in the movie). Malagasy believe lemurs carry the souls of their ancestors and are considered sacred animals that are deeply revered by the people.

Andrianampoinimerinatompokoindrindra. Ladies and gentlemen, this is a name, of a person. To be precise, it's the name of a 19th century king of Madagascar. According to Malagasy tradition, every part of a name carries a meaning and is joined to form one name with no separation between the first and second/family name. For instance the former King's name, mentioned above (*too long to retype*), means 'the prince who was born to Imerina and who is my real lord'.

Another example of a mouthful name is that of the Former President – who reigned during our stay in Madagascar – His excellency Hery Martial Rajaonarimampianina Rakotoarimanana.

Similarly, Razafindrandriatsimaniry is a 24-letter sentence (*sorry, name*) that means 'the grandson of the prince or nobleman who is envious of no one.' (I am personally not too envious of that name.) Long names are not only given to people but also to proper nouns like cities. The capital city of Madagascar is Antananarivo which is mercifully shortened to just 'Tana'.

Although predominantly Christians, most Malagasy people hold on to their respective traditions and superstitions. They strongly believe in their ancestors, magic powers and taboos, also known as *fady*.

The *Famidihana* is a very popular and significant celebration where family members dig dead bodies out of the graves. The remains are unwrapped and rewrapped in large silk scarves called *Lamba* before they (the relatives) dance around the skeleton and take pictures with the dead (selfies are allowed too). Also known as 'turning of the bones', this practice is carried out in September every two to seven years after the person departs this life. In so doing, Malagasy people believe they are maintaining links with their ancestors who, according to them, play a vital role in their daily lives. Note: the Malagasy find it extremely impolite to make negative comments on this practice.

Having twins is often celebrated with great joy and

considered a blessing in most parts of Africa. However, the opposite is true in certain remote areas of Madagascar. According to an ancient belief amongst the 'Antambahoaka' people, twins are a malediction and raising them brings misfortune or even death to the families. Women who give birth to twins must abandon one or both twins, to do so, they are often taken out into the bush and left to die. Failure to do so will lead to rejection by the community. Fortunately, civilisation is penetrating these rural areas and most of the 'unwanted' twins end up in centres and orphanages where they are put up for adoption.

After a woman gives birth, the placenta and newborn's umbilical cord are passed on to the father whose responsibility is to bury them under a stone at the entrance of their rural ancestral home. This is different in the urban areas where the umbilical cord is now buried in the house somewhere safe and clean. The father must not look back after the cord is buried. The belief is that the new-born whose umbilical cord is lost or not buried in the proper way will grow up to be a forgetful adult.

Some Malagasy believe that a baby's hair should only be cut when they are three months old. The 'Ala-volo' is a hair cutting ceremony where a family member with beautiful hair is invited to cut the baby's hair. The cut hair is then put on a large bowl and mixed with honey and sweet potatoes before it's eaten by the family members. This signifies a rite of passage for the baby to fully integrate into society. *Fancy a hairy sweet potato pie?*

Each day of the week is favourable for a particular purpose. Thursday is considered the first day in the Malagasy calendar and a good day to start off any long-term goals such as construction of a house or starting a business. It isn't recommended to organise a burial on a Thursday lest it becomes the starting point of a series of consecutive deaths within the family.

Malagasy respect certain rituals when constructing a house. A house should be built facing west, where the sun sets. Windows should be located north and doors should face west. Everything inside the house should also be positioned in the right place. They believe that the North is where wealth, holiness and happiness come from.

The only staple for Malagasy cuisine is rice and the verb for eating a meal is *Mihinam-bary*, which literally translates to 'eat rice'. In most families, rice is consumed for breakfast, lunch and dinner. 'Ranovola' is a special tea in Madagascar; this tea is actually burnt rice water. It's prepared by burning rice in a pan and then boiling the water over the burnt rice which is strained and enjoyed as morning tea. It's quite the acquired taste.

Comoros Islands

THE UNION OF COMOROS is a small Island in the Indian Ocean with a rich cultural blend of African, Arab and European influences. The common languages used on the islands are French, Comorian, Arabic, and Swahili. Islam is the dominant religion, and deeply influences Comoros' culture and traditions. Customs and religious celebrations are respected and provide the framework for daily life.

Predominantly Muslim, there are numerous mosques spread over the island. Our home was surrounded by four mosques, all with loud speakers that simultaneously called the faithful to prayer. The 4am calls were the hardest for us specially during the first few months of living on the Island but we eventually got used to it.

The Comoros Islands emerged from a volcanic activity from the floor of the Indian Ocean and has had its share of volcanic eruptions. Some volcanoes are small and others large – the highest peak is Mount Karthala – an active volcano with a height of 2,361 metres (7,746 feet) above sea level. Mount Karthala has experienced 20 active volcanoes in the past two centuries and continues to be active. The last eruption recorded was 2007. Despite the volcanic activity, Karthala is a magnificent landscape with unique flora and fauna.

This small Island is nicknamed 'Coup-Coup Islands' due to the series of coups and counter coups it has endured since its independence from France over 40 years ago. Comoros has seen over 20 coups d'état or attempted coups that have led to the assassination of various heads of state including the first president Ahmed Abdallah. If you do the maths, they have had on average a coup almost every two years.

Even though they have over the last decade experienced relative stability and peace, the past political turbulence and poor infrastructural development are some of the reasons the islands haven't been etched on the global tourist circuit. They remain unexposed despite their unrivalled marine paradise that offers one of the world's highest concentration of coral reefs, crystal blue waters, sandy beaches and dense vegetation.

Traditional Comorian women wear brightly coloured fabrics called 'Shiromani', and paint their faces with a ground sandalwood and coral paste called 'msindanu' which they claim protects them from the sun. Many women slap this 'Sun Protection Factor' paste on their faces and go about their daily business out and about town. One morning while at the fish market, I observed a lady who got me chuckling. Standing at her fish stall, she was clad in the traditional Shiromani with a head veil and her face completely caked in the 'msindanu' SPF paste and in one hand she casually held a lit cigarette and in the other hand a sharp knife, clearly ready to slice up the huge, freshly fished barracuda in front of her. There was something powerful about this image. I was itching to take a picture but Comorians believe it's bad luck to have their photos taken by strangers.

In Grande Comore (the biggest of the three Islands), people get married in two ceremonies; *Le Petit Mariage* (small wedding) and *Le Grand Mariage* (grand wedding). The latter is nothing short of a spectacle that involves entire communities and can last for as long as three weeks. With high poverty levels, an underdeveloped infrastructure and a population of under one million people scattered around the three Islands, *le Grand Mariage* is a major event that contributes to (or depletes) the economy. Comorians save up, collect from family members and communities, and some will take out bank loans or spend their entire life's earnings on the wedding. A *Grand Mariage* can cost between $40,000 to $80,000. The groom's family pays for all the festivities, provides dowry, silks and a whole lot of gold jewellery worth tens of thousands of dollars for the bride. And the bride's family takes care of building the couple's home, although ownership will solely be for the wife-to-be, which means the house remains the property of the wife even after divorce (*she keeps the gold of course)*.

A 'Grand Marriage' is a fundamental cultural institution and a major stage in the customary life of an individual that holds significant social importance. Once accomplished, the husband is considered to be a *Grand Notable*. He obtains a notability status that's considered to be the highest social level, a title that accords him the power to participate and contribute to public affairs concerning his community. A *Grand Notable* can be recognised from his attire; he wears special ceremonial clothing with a special scarf on Fridays. In some villages, he enters the mosque through a special door where he is given a specific seat at the front.

Apart from the social status and respect, the grand wedding is an investment that guarantees a certain economic security. He is invited to all wedding ceremonies of his community and is frequently awarded cash envelopes for every upcoming wedding. *Nice way to recoup those thousands!*

These weddings are a factor of social cohesion and a form of redistribution of wealth that comes with social pressure for most firstborn girls to get married because of the wealth it brings to the family and community. Tradition has it that any man of age with the financial capacity can take a customary wife (preferably from the same village as him in order to keep the 'wealth' within the family). This island has small communities and marriages between cousins (distant or close) is a common thing. Another downside is since it's a community obligation to contribute towards these weddings, it's financially burdensome for families with limited income.

Women enjoy a social status as owners of the couple's home because a married woman is given a house and land which is passed down to the eldest daughter. The domestic unit is dominated by the mother's relatives (or children from earlier marriages). Married couples and their children live with the wife's parents and females often remain part of their mother's 'household' even after marriage.

When she loses her husband, a widow is expected to stay indoors for a mourning period of four months and ten days, this is called 'idani'. Only her family members are allowed to visit and bring her food. If she must go out in public, she must dress up in white clothing that covers her head all the way down to her feet and speak in a very low tone during this period.

The rite of circumcision is an important stage in a young boy's life between two and nine years. It calls for a two-day celebration that includes prayer and making a sacrifice.

Similarly, when a young girl gets her first period the news is announced to all family and friends who congratulate her. In Anjouan (one of the Islands), the young girl is pampered for several days. She is put on a special diet; soups and spicy broth and entitled to daily body massages with coconut oil *(I was born in the wrong country, ha*!). She cannot step out of the house during her first period and at the end of her period, a purification shower is performed by the oldest member of the family followed by a prayer and a festive ceremony called 'pondzo'. It's customary in both cases, (the boy's circumcision and the girl's first period) for the guests to bring a gift.

It's probable that the perfume you use or the cloves that spice up your cookies and the vanilla that flavours your ice cream comes from Comoros. The Comoros have been famously called the 'perfumed islands' due to their abundance of fragrant plant life. The islands have three main exports; Cloves, Vanilla (vanilla aficionados say that the world's best *vanille bourbon* is found in the Comoros). They are the world's largest producer of Ylang-ylang, a flower from which essential oils are extracted for the production of many fragrant oils and perfumes. This sweet and floral smelling flower is in fact the base of the famous Chanel N° 5 perfume.

Apart from its use in perfumes, the essential oil derived from ylang-ylang has plenty of medicinal values and is often used in aromatherapy, anti-depressants, antiseptic and aphrodisiac properties. So, if you want to boost your romantic mood while on your honeymoon in Comoros, ylang-ylang could be a solution (wink).

Life begins at the end of your comfort zone.

— NEALE D. WALSCH

AFTERWORD
HOME

/həʊm/

ACCORDING TO our trusted friends Google and Wikipedia, the word 'Home' can mean:

1. A place where one lives permanently, especially as a member of a family or household.
2. The family or social unit occupying a permanent residence.
3. Place of residence, accommodation, property, roof over one's head, lodging, quarters, abode, dwelling, (informal) digs, pad, domicile, abode, dwelling
4. Native land, homeland, home town, birthplace, roots, fatherland, motherland, mother country, country of origin, land of one's fathers.
5. The finishing point in a race.

As we conclude these expat tales, we find it increasingly difficult to define where and what 'HOME' is. It's neither definition 1, nor 2. 3 and 4 are close enough to what 'home' means for us but what resonates most with us is that good ol' cliche – 'Home is where the heart is'.

Change is always hard. But it takes gumption to live a life of having to regularly relocate to unfamiliar places and be separated from close friends and family. Expat life may seem like a dream life; and in many ways, it is. I mean, very few people would resist a chance to travel around the world with tickets paid for by the employer, have the opportunity to learn a new language, immerse themselves in new and fascinating cultures, have kids attend international schools, live in housing that is often better than what they have back in their home countries, have access to a driver, a nanny, housekeeper and meet interesting people that they would normally not meet while living their everyday life back home. That's some of the exciting stuff about being an expatriate. But there's also the non-exciting stuff and it can leave you questioning whether any of the exciting stuff is at all worth it.

An expatriate existence can be mentally, emotionally and physically challenging, disruptive, shocking and downright exhausting. For starters, there is the constant feeling of not belonging. It's never your culture, your language, your neighbours, your house, your car. Sometimes the only thing that's truly yours is your family and the clothes on your back. Everything else rotates and revolves every couple of years and you lose track of which house was cosier, which friendship was more meaningful or which one was real or not, what the name of your kid's last 'best friend' in school was, which address you lived on last and which country was most fulfilling.

We have cried many ugly tears at the emptiness that engulfs us at times. We have felt insecure and have doubted ourselves over our decisions, especially those involving the children; Is the school right for them? How will all this moving affect them in future? Will they turn out all right?

We often feel we neither belong to our birth country of Uganda nor to our adopted ones of Belgium and France. When we travel back to Uganda, Belgium or France, we call that a holiday because despite the fact that we are nationals of these countries, we find ourselves transient in them too, staying there for just a few weeks or months, visiting relatives and friends before moving onto our next work posting.

This affects not only us but the friendships we have in those countries. Many of our friends and family back home can never really imagine or understand the stories we tell them about where we live because to them, the countries we live in are so far off their radar, entirely removed from their everyday lives. Many of our relatives and friends have lived in the same country since birth, occupied the same house since getting married or having children, they've had the same circle of friends and the closest they have come to witnessing a war is when there is a town protest over the colour of the Christmas tree lighting. They only see the stuff we see, on their television, in the comfort of their living rooms.

With this difference in thought, you feel you almost can't relate to them and neither can they to you. This, of course, is in no way meant to derogate them and doesn't change the way we feel about friendships that are well-cemented. It does however change some of the dynamics, and we often find ourselves more drawn to people with life experiences that are similar to ours.

Today, where relocations are more common, staying in touch via email and other social media is much easier. However, in countries like China, most Western social media is banned. This, plus the dreaded hour difference, makes it pretty hard to catch up or keep up with our loved ones. Many times, we have wanted to pick up the phone and call family or friends in another part of the world, before realising that it's the middle of the night where they are while early morning birds are happily chirping away from where we are.

Through it all, we come away extremely appreciative of the incredible beauty and wonder we have seen in the world. We have relished every good and bad moment. Every challenge has made us appreciate our own resilience. And we sure as heck have lapped-up those luxurious moments we would otherwise not have experienced in a 'normal' life.

We have learned a few hacks on how to acclimatise to our transient surroundings; Mixing with like-minded people and the locals, immersing ourselves in the new culture, learning the local lingo, clutching onto the authenticity of what and who we truly are, and just learning to be oh-so-thankful; Thankful for the cities we have visited and have lived in, the people we have met, the foods we have tasted, the schools our children have attended, the friends they have made and the resilience they have gained from it all.

It sure isn't hunky dory all the time but what an absolute honour it is to see the world like this.

The biggest lesson from all these travels? Never judge a book (country in this case) by its cover.

PS do not judge this book's cover either. ;-)

ACKNOWLEDGEMENTS

SPECIAL THANKS to the Kasujja and Epenu families. These are large African families so to mention each and every one of you by name would take us a year (and a whole other book) to write. Thanks to our other families; the Roberts and the Van de Veldes.

Many thanks to those who gave us invaluable guidance and feedback; Anita Ogaa, Mina Yan, Stella Angwalas-Huson, Rebecca Nassali, Aude Ndabaneze Ofungi, Saïlïfa Nzwalo, Kenneth Ntulume, Aileen Boy and our fellow 'suspect' Paddy Siyanga-Knudsen.

To the friends who knew us before these expat journeys began and who remain huge parts of our lives. Although we all seem to be scattered around the world – Uganda, The United States of America, United Kingdom, Germany, France, Italy, Canada and many other countries – the distance has not affected our bond. We love you.

Last but not least, to each and every person we have met throughout these meandering world routes.

Thank you.

PEARL KASUJJA-VAN DE VELDE

PEARL GREW UP in the small, quiet town of Entebbe, Uganda. Here, she spent a carefree life before a wandering Belgian man plucked her away and barged her into a nomadic expat existence. With this new life, her first book idea was born and, together with her insanely hilarious and fellow expat-wife and friend Julie, the idea turned into these pages. She lives all over the world with her husband and two girls but home is Uganda and Belgium. When she's not writing, she enjoys travelling, yoga, tennis, music and chicken wings.

 facebook.com/pearl.kasujja

 instagram.com/pearl_kasujja

JULIE EPENU-ROBERT

BORN AND RAISED IN UGANDA, Julie has called seven countries "Home" for the past eighteen years. She is currently an islander living in the Comoros Islands with her husband and their four "children" (two humans and two furry creatures). When she isn't writing or reading, she is honing her craft and growing her small handmade business. In theory, she is focused on achieving her dreams but in reality, she is probably playing Monopoly with her children. Besides travel, she enjoys tennis, dancing, nature walks and a good laugh.